Hindsight

ALSO BY MARYANNE COMAROTO

SKINNY, TAN & RICH
Unveiling the Myth

Hindsight

What You Need to Know
Before You Drop Your Drawers!

MARYANNE
COMAROTO

Bridge the Gap Publishing
A Division of INNER~tainment, LLC
Greenbrae, CA

Published by: Bridge the Gap Publishing,
a division of INNER~tainment, LLC
336 Bon Air Center, Suite 124 | Greenbrae, CA 94904
http://www.maryannelive.com

ISBN 10: 0-9746610-0-7
ISBN 13: 978-0-9746610-0-1
Library of Congress Control Number 2009921205

Edited by Eve Hogan
Cover and Interior Design by Dotti Albertine
Published in the United States of America

For Nat

Contents

Acknowledgments

My list is long, so there is little hope of being brief. I have learned that gratitude is a portal for joy, and it is my earnest desire that my words wrap warmly around the hearts of those who have loved me, and, most of all, wanted me to rise to the highest version of myself.

First, thank you to all the ladies in my book for offering their stories of heartbreak and healing. Some suffered, some lost their lives, and others are still trying to find and heal their hearts; thank you from the bottom of mine. It has been an honor to speak for, and on behalf of, you who have felt the pain of separation and loss—loss of self and loss of innocence. Your selflessness for the greater good is grand.

For David, my beloved, my husband and my incredibly tolerant comrade, thank you for being a genuine gentleman and not a fake one. I swear, if were a man, I would want to be just like you (except with slightly less hair). The fact that you understand there is no "we" without "me" is nothing less than miraculous and the best gift you could have given me, besides the gift of your presence. Without hesitation, you have exceeded my reach for the moon. I can only vaguely remember life without you!

My son, who makes everything count and matter deeply. It is such a privilege being your mom! You are fiercely true to yourself and equally self-effacing. Thank you for your uncompromising sensitivity and willingness to tell the truth despite the consequences. I am certain I could not love anyone more than I love you.

My editor and friend, Eve, you are, no doubt, a goddess and a most gracious warrior. No matter how full your life, you have always made room for me. I have yet to determine what I ever did to be the recipient of such unconditional love. Thank you a million times for your gentle encouragement, sound expertise and lifetime of devotion to your own winding path. I love, love, love you so big!

Gabrielle, thank you for inspiring me to be the best version of myself, for agreeing to support my vision to help end some degree of human suffering, for taking the time to write the foreword for this book, and for only ever seeing the real me! There has never been any doubt I love you.

My brother Peter and his devoted wife, Sandy, your courage the carriage making your relationship and marriage an inspiration to us all.

Shakti, your devotion is the shore on which my journey as a writer unforgettably began. No words have been born to describe my thankfulness.

My teacher Kathy A. Thank you from the top of my head to tips of my toes for inspiring me to stay on my path. I love being your student and so admire your genuine humility.

Doug, you are impeccable and true. God bless you always for inviting me to quit my day job, find my voice and follow my deepest intuition.

Karen, my friend, your heart is big enough for the world to melt inside. Thank you for wearing it on your sleeve. I wish you every happiness. You deserve nothing less.

Judy, my soul sister, thank you for your open arms and heart, for the genuine invitation to be chosen family. And for always encouraging me to keep my eye on the ball, however many times I wanted to close up shop and open a boutique.

Gayle, thank you for reminding me life is a beach, not a race to be won. I am so thrilled and proud to be, among other things, your semi-Jewish friend. And, to your precious husband, Jayme, my brother from another mother, thank you for your enthusiastic support and heartfelt advice. You are unabashedly fun, and I love you for it!

Anila, my right (and sometimes left) arm. Without you I am a hypervigilant, warp-speed nightmare. You are a master far beyond the office, and a being who I admire and care for deeply. Thank you for all that you do every day that makes our little part of the world go 'round—I am truly grateful.

Karen and Bojana, what a wild and exciting ride! Thank you for your commitment, for being mindful of the things that really matter and for your remarkable elegance.

And my gracious appreciation for the rest of my editing team, Heidi, Netty and Melissa. Without you I would have been lost in a sea of phonetics and run-on sentences, caught in a word storm with an empty quill. Dotti, my book would be naked without you. Always, I love and value your artistic panache.

My mother, one of my greatest, if not *the* greatest, teachers. Thank you for pushing up against the norm, for risking it all to make a better life for us, for leading the way down the path of personal growth. If it weren't for all you have endured, I would not likely feel so free to speak, with such passion, my own truth. I love you, Mom.

All my other friends and family who I have not mentioned: I am uncharacteristically at a loss for words to express my sincere jubilation for the celebration my life has become as a result of loving, being loved by and knowing you—one and all.

To Mother Father, The Divine, your promises have stood the test of time. "Know thy self and the truth shall set you free." No greater words spoken. Jesus, you healed my heart; Mary, you resurrected my soul; Buddha, you freed my mind. There is no possible way I will attempt to list all that I am grateful for here, but I will say this: Because of *you*, I am that!

Foreword

By Gabrielle Roth

I grew up trusting that everyone else (especially men) would have The Answers for me. Then, as the song says, "I took my problems to the dance floor" and began to develop a body of work called the 5Rhythms, which became the map to everything I've ever needed to know.

As my work evolved, it became clear to me that all of us—men, women, all variations—had been duped into living a straitjacketed existence, trapped by an imbalance of spirit and flesh that has dominated Western civilization for at least two thousand years. I began to seek deeper than gender for the roots of this imbalance and found them in the lack of respect we had for all things feminine. My work has been to bring forward a feminine style of spirituality that also honors the masculine. As Taoist philosopher Lao Tzu counseled, "Know the masculine, but stay with the feminine." In my world, everything flows from the instinctive, intuitive wisdom of the body; and I have learned that when we stop listening to it we are driven, by outside influences, into choices that have nothing to do with our truth. The body is our spiritual path.

I first met Maryanne on the dance floor years ago, both of us moving to the music as if our lives depended on it (they do). The first thing I noticed about her was her inner light, and the second thing I noticed was how directly and clearly she let it shine on everyone around her. We became fast friends. To this day, her intelligence is moving, swift and aimed at the heart of the matter, and her curiosity is seductive, contagious and engaging.

In Maryanne, truth moves inside an organic vulnerability we all hunger for, even though we have been conditioned to keep all that we see, feel and think under the radar and behind the smile. But not my lady, not my friend! In Maryanne's presence, one is immediately grounded in an intimate, loving, generous and piercingly truthful field. She cracks the code, and she will help you do the same. The questions she offers are real, nitty-gritty ones that we all think of but rarely say aloud; their answers will make all the difference in your romantic choices. In *Hindsight* you will discover a subtle interplay of frankness and elegance that reveals the questions you need to answer and the answers you need to question. Maryanne, as goddess and guide, weaves her story of suffering and transformation into a deep and profound love story. She falls in love with herself, as many have fallen before her, and she reaches out from that place within herself to offer us a hand truly connected to its tender, wild heart.

Fairy tales can become real—just keep your warrior sister's questionnaires emblazoned in the back of your brain!

—GABRIELLE ROTH
Manhattan, December 2008

Introduction

Real love stories never have endings.
—RICHARD BACH

I was in L.A. some years ago, a new author about to speak at my first conference. My publicist, Veronica, had never seen me speak in public and was, like a new mommy, a bit worried. During her pep talk she mentioned no less than three times that I should keep it light, that people want to be entertained and feel good; they like happy stories, etc, etc. I told her not to worry.

I was the third to speak that morning, and by the time I approached the podium the audience had thinned considerably. There were only a few folks left, scattered among the chairs, taking a rest or checking their cell phones. She told me not to worry or take it personally, that it was probably just as well, since I was cutting my teeth as a speaker.

The outdoor venue lent a lighthearted feel to the Relationship Convention: hundreds of people were flitting hopefully from one booth to the next, seeking love advice, solutions, lotions, potions and magic answers. There were tarot readers, psychics, motivational speakers and healers, angel card readers and psychiatrists all peddling their secrets to love and relationships. And then there was me.

I was not a headliner, but the title of my book was intriguing: *Skinny, Tan and Rich: Unveiling the Myth.* I was supposed to talk about what a "good girl handbook" was, which I had alluded to in my book.

I had a better idea.

"Welcome and thank you for coming!" I announced with unbridled passion to the few people in the audience, one of whom was actually facing me. You'd have thought I was the M.C. for the Academy Awards. "My name is Maryanne Comaroto and I'm running for President . . . Just kidding, just wanted to see if you were here yet!"

One of my favorite things to do before I gave a talk was to wait for everyone to "get here." I had heard about a tribe in Africa that greeted each other by asking, "Are you here yet?" And then they would wait—as I was happy to do. And I did. Then I explained that getting here was part of how you can get what you came for. "If you aren't here, how can you get what you came for? How can I give it to you?" A few more people sat down, then a few more.

"Would you raise your hand if you have an empty seat next to you?" Several people looked right and left and a few raised their hands. I felt like a carnie trying to get people's attention. "Come on, raise your hand if you see an empty seat!" More and more folks took a seat.

I continued. "This morning I read a disturbing article about fifteen women who were slain by their lovers. I ask if the seat next to you is empty, because I wonder if one of our sisters could have been sitting next to you instead of being dead. If only she knew what I know now, and what I am about to share with you."

I looked over at Veronica, whose eyes were bulging out of her publicist head, and I knew she was hoping I wouldn't say "dead" one more time. Okay, so this wasn't exactly *light*, but I was going somewhere, and she was coming with me.

More people drizzled in, wondering what all the fuss and buzz was about—my voice would have carried even without a microphone. "That was the gruesome headline: fifteen different women killed by their lovers," I said, walking out toward the folks standing. "And then I thought, *Wait a minute, I can do something about it. Maybe I can help stop this from ever happening to another person.*

"Okay, raise your hand if you're in a relationship." Half the people raised their hands. "Raise your hand if you're single." Several more people raised their hands.

"Sir, I noticed you didn't raise your hand. First time on the planet?" I asked, with a smile that showed that I meant no harm.

He smiled, a bit taken aback. "No."

"So, are you in a relationship or are you single?" I asked, putting my hand on his shoulder and him on the spot. "I have a wife," he said, nervously.

"Well, in case no one has mentioned it, being married means that you are in a relationship." Light laughter rippled through the crowd as I patted his shoulder and walked back to the front of the audience.

"Really, you might be surprised. You think this question is difficult—you should see how hard it is to answer a question when we want the juicy part, when there's a little intimate chemistry mixed in. Chemistry can make it hard to think clearly. 'Who is this other person?' These are things that we just honestly don't think about, right?"

The place was filled up over halfway now, as more folks stood around the edge of the venue. Veronica looked curious but calm. I carried on. "I mean, when we hook up, most of us aren't really thinking too much about what can go wrong. Oh, we all have our laundry list, but for the most part we are looking to be in love, to finding our soul mate or some companionship. That's what this symposium is all about . . . relationships, love, right? Well, how is it that fifteen of our sisters aren't here today? What did they miss? What didn't they know before they got involved with Mr. Absolutely Wrong? Today *we* have the privilege of paying attention; right now, everyone here is on the right side of the ground. So just take a moment and think about this: What didn't our sisters know, that if they had known, they might be with us today? What, in hindsight, might we have had to offer?"

The only sounds for about fifteen seconds were a few birds and an airplane flying overhead. I started down the center aisle.

"Okay, you can put your hands down now, thank you," I said, lightening up the mood a bit since no one had their hand up. I looked over at Veronica. She winked. "So, wow, heavy," I continued. "Well that's the choice we get to make every day. We have been blessed with free will and, well, gang, let's get to it. Let's practice today asking each other some great questions. Let's practice finding out things about each other *before* we get intimate, *before* we drop our drawers. Because, well . . . we can!

"Excuse me, sir," I said, walking toward the tall man standing all the way in the back with his arms folded. The place was packed now, standing room only. "Are you twenty-one, sir?"

"Yeah," he said, barely audible.

I skipped up to him. "Are you twenty-one, sir?" I asked again, as if I were carding him. I put the microphone to his mouth.

"Yes," he answered again, slightly amused. The people in the front rows swiveled around a bit to see him.

"Really? 'Cause you don't look twenty-one," I said, playing with him. I turned to the audience. "Well, he says he's twenty-one. Should we believe him?"

I walked over to a young woman sitting down. "Should we believe him?" I asked, offering her the microphone.

"Sure, I guess," she said shyly.

"What's your name?"

"Theresa."

I looked back at the man, who still had his arms folded. "Theresa says we should believe that you're twenty-one." I walked up the aisle. "Well, I'm not convinced. Why should we believe him? 'Cause he says so? 'Cause Theresa says so?" I looked around. "Okay, I'll bet you a dollar he's not twenty-one. Come on . . . Anybody? Surely, *someone* wants to win a dollar!" I saw a man in the front row raise his hand and scurried over to him. "Okay, we have a bet. One dollar." I shook the gentleman's hand and walked back to the man with folded arms.

"What's your name?" I smiled.

"Ted."

"Okay, Ted, let me see your driver's license." I held out my hand. He looked at me and then toward his buddy, who goaded him on. "You're sure you wanna do this?" I asked. "There's hard cash on the table betting that you're not twenty-one, Ted." I put the mic up to his mouth.

He smiled, reached for his wallet and flipped it open, handing me his ID. "Ooooh, just as I suspected, He's NOT twenty-one. Ha!" I skipped off toward the man who took the bet.

"Sir, you have lost the dollar, because he's thirty-two," I laughed. The crowd groaned and chuckled.

"That's a great example of what can happen when we ask something and the person assumes they know what we're really asking. Ted, Theresa and the man who took the bet all assumed I meant 'Is Ted *at least* twenty-one.' But my question was, 'Is Ted twenty-one?'

"Anyway, the easy questions are ones like, 'How old are you? Where are you from? What do you do?' Then it can get a little harder, as we get beyond the formalities. We already saw how confusing 'Are you in a relationship?' can be, and that wasn't even asked with sex on the line." I smiled again at the man who had taken a while to claim his marriage. "Let's not underplay the long list of things we need to know. For example…sir, yes you, sir, hi!" I said putting the mic to a late-twenties fella's face.

"Hi," he said, leaning down into the mic.

"What's your name?"

"Josh."

"Okay, hi, Josh . . . Sooo, Josh, have you ever been in jail or shot heroin?" I stood there with an enormous smile on my face. He laughed and wasn't sure if I actually expected him to answer.

"No, really, Josh, have you ever been in jail or . . . yeah . . . shot heroin . . . ever?" I folded my arms and waited for him to answer.

"No," he said.

"No, you've never been in jail, Josh? Come on!"

"Okay, well, I've never shot heroin," he admitted, and we all laughed. I was delighted with myself and jumped up and down, and then off into the now-packed audience.

"Theresa, where are you? Theresa, have you ever been in jail?" I asked making my way over to her, and holding out the microphone.

"No," she said blushing.

"How do we know?" I said half kidding. She looked at me more seriously. "Okay, I know your mother's here somewhere, Theresa. We'll let you off this time, but do you see what I mean? We have to ask something we really want to know about each other, so we feel a bit safer to get vulnerable.

"Come on people! When do you want to know, for example, that your new love interest has escaped from prison—before or after you get intimate?" I scanned the audience. "Seriously. When do you want to know that your partner has a crack habit—before or after you move in together, before or after he or she cleans out your bank account? When do you want to know if your boyfriend has ever beaten a woman, or is on the list of child abusers or has ever killed anyone? Before or after he does it to you?"

I looked around.

"Where's Josh? Is he still . . . there he is." I quickly walked toward Josh. "Josh, when do you want to know that your new girlfriend robs banks—before or after she ties you up and threatens to castrate you?" Everyone laughed. "Okay Josh, you think this is funny, tell me you don't know what I am talking about? Come on, I know you have a story. Heck, we're close now, we all know you've been in jail. How ugly could this be?" I smiled. He laughed, and off he went with a sordid story of discovering way too late something that—in hindsight—he should have asked, should have noticed or should have paid attention to before he dropped his drawers.

As I walked away from the podium I knew something had to be done. As a culture we are not getting it. That I had dodged death myself, but fifteen more had not, illustrated only one of the simple truths I had discovered the hard way: If we don't care for ourselves, we will not likely be true to ourselves or notice if we are running straight toward red flags. Never mind taking care to approach other people with a set of tools guaranteed to help attract a healthy, fulfilling, sustainable relationship. Instead, because we are so desperate to be loved—to not be alone *out there* in the cold, cruel world—we will do whatever we have to do, say whatever we have to say, to have someone love us. We will overlook the most obvious warnings and red flags, thus setting ourselves up to repeat the same pattern we have programmed, falling deeper into hopelessness and despair.

And by my calculations, every day women just like you have sex with a man because they don't have the self-esteem to say no, because they so desperately want to be loved or don't want to be alone!

WHO NEEDS TO READ THIS BOOK?

Hindsight is for all of you who think you must be someone you are not so you can attract and sustain great love; for you who believe that you must be flawless, poised, and low-maintenance to have a great relationship. It's for you who have bought or been sold the story that, by nature, humans are not monogamous; that pornography is art; and that a penis actually has a mind of its own. For all of you who believe that he (or she) didn't call because they're "too busy"; that because you had sex means you're in a relationship, and that your new sexual partner is actually going to leave their spouse to be with you. It's for you fairy-tale royalty who secretly still hope and pray that you will be swept off your feet. It's for you who choose partners with the expectation that they will change; for you who keep making poor choices in partners without asking enough of the right questions. This book is for you who have come to rationalize inappropriate behavior as a way of life.

For some of you this guide will reaffirm what you already know; it

STATISTICS ON INTIMATE VIOLENCE

- Every day in the U.S., five to eleven women are killed by a male intimate partner.[1]

- Between 2,100,100 and 8,000,000 women are abused by their partners annually in the U.S. At least once every fifteen seconds, a woman is beaten by her husband or boyfriend.[2]

- The Surgeon General has reported for at least ten years that battering is the single largest cause of injury to U.S. women.[3]

- 21-30 percent of college students report at least one occurrence of physical assault with a dating partner.[4]

- 15.4 percent of gay men, 11.4 percent of lesbians and 7.7 percent of heterosexual men, are assaulted by a date or intimate partner during their lives.[5]

- More than 1 million women and 371,000 men are stalked by partners each year.[6]

- One out of four women in the United States has been physically assaulted or raped by an intimate partner; one out of 14 men also reported such experiences.[7]

- According to Rutgers University the background characteristics of people entering a marriage/relationship have major implications for their risk of divorce, with high annual income and having a first child born within 24 months of the wedding being low risk factors.[8]

- Today, there are approximately one million people living with HIV/AIDS in the U.S. The impact of HIV on younger women is particularly notable. More than six in ten new HIV infections among women (including white, black, and Latina) were among those aged thirteen through thirty-nine in 2006. 32 percent were between the ages of thirteen and twenty-nine, and 31 percent were aged thirty to thirty-nine.[9]

- One in four teenage girls—3,200,000—has a sexually transmitted disease (STD).[10]

- During their lifetime, women attempt suicide two to three times as often as men. Among females, those in their 40s and 50s have the highest rate of suicide (rate 7.53 per 100,000 population).[11]

For sources of this information, please see page 179.

will give you the chance to brush up on your relationship skills—which, for me, is always of value. (Even for the know-it-all I can be, there is always room for growth). Or perhaps this book will provide an opportunity for you to refresh some skills that you find you need right now, or it will remind you of a gem you have forgotten you have. For others, this may be the first time you will be introduced to these concepts, practices and exercises. Regardless of the category you fall into, wherever you find yourself right now, stay tuned! "Survey says" most of us need an overhaul here. I know I did, and I have worked hard every day to stay on my path of personal development, to "stay awake."

— *Relationship Quiz* —

Before you take another step, take a moment for yourself and see if your behavior or beliefs might be standing between you and your heart's desire.

Answer "True" or "False" to each of the following statements:

_____ Happily Ever After is real and possible.

_____ Something is wrong with me.

_____ Chemistry is an indicator of love.

_____ If I'm having sex, I'm in a relationship.

_____ A man's penis has a mind of its own.

_____ Men are dogs.

_____ I can change a man if I'm the right woman.

_____ I could die of a broken heart.

_____ I have to be beautiful or perfect to attract a man.

_____ All the good ones are taken.

_____ Good guys are boring.

_____ Men don't like powerful women.

_____ If we didn't have intercourse, we didn't really have sex.

_____ I was drunk, so I'm not responsible.

_____ I wasn't married so I wasn't cheating.

_____ Money can buy you love.

_____ I have to say yes even when I want to say no.

_____ I smile even when I want to scream.

_____ I fake orgasms.

_____ All men really want one thing.

_____ I need a man.

_____ I have sex when I want to be held.

_____ I give even when I only want to be taken care of.

_____ I pretend I am someone I am not.

_____ I fear that I am unlovable or not lovable enough.

_____ I don't need skills to have a relationship.

_____ Love is a feeling.

_____ No relationship is perfect.

_____ I just haven't met the right guy yet.

_____ Men can't handle the truth about a woman's past.

_____ He'll settle down once we have kids.

_____ If I have sex, there's a better chance of having a relationship.

_____ Just because a man cheated before doesn't mean he will cheat with me.

_____ The right woman can make a man change.

_____ Men need sex before they will commit.

_____ If I hang in there long enough, he'll eventually ask me to marry him.

_____ Men mature later in life.

_____ Men are not good listeners.

_____ Men are on their best behavior until I have sex with them.

_____ Men think sex is the most important part of a relationship.

_____ I have to lure a man into relationship.

_____ I have to manipulate men to get them and what I want.

_____ Men don't want to hear about my bad feelings.

_____ Men don't want a high-maintenance gal.

_____ I have to play the game to get the guy.

_____ All men cheat; it's how they are wired.

_____ Men are biologically more sexually driven than women.

_____ Men don't want to talk about anything deep.

_____ Men think I should simply be happy no matter what they do.

If you answered "True" to any of these statements, you should definitely read this book! If you have *ever* answered "True" to any of these statements, almost answered "True" to any of these statements, know someone who might answer "True," might answer "True" yourself someday; if your daughter answered "True"; your granddaughter or your sister answered "True"; your mother, your friend, your baby sister's niece, your boyfriend's ex-girlfriend, your mother-in-law, the lady in the grocery store checkout line, your yoga teacher, golf partner, or stockbroker—in fact, if you can read, you should read this book. It might save someone's life, perhaps your own. The wisdom in it saved mine!

SHATTERING THE FAIRY TALES

Growing up, my relationship role models were Lady and the Tramp, Cinderella and the Flintstones. While my parents didn't quite make the G-rated list, their relationship would have been rated, well, further toward the P-for-passionate end of the alphabet. Like most people, they wanted primarily to love and be loved, as did their parents and theirs before them. Nature and nurture aside, the pursuit of Happily Ever After was an American institution that intoxicated us all.

Not yet drunk from it, by the time I was in kindergarten I had figured out that there was something fishy about all those fairy tales. On one particular Valentine's Day, when love was abounding, I asked why I couldn't have two…okay, *three* . . . valentines at the same time. I was told it had something to do with cows and free milk, which clearly made no sense to me. My father, on the other hand, didn't speak in metaphors; he said that all men wanted was one thing, and that would make me a whore. At the ripe age of five, I wondered what a "whore" was and why it was bad. But I realized that polygamy wasn't okay for a girl.

Despite warnings from Command Central about becoming a dairy queen/Ho, my role models evolved from kindergarten to high school. Instead of Wilma Flintstone, there was Natalie Wood as Gypsy Rose Lee; instead of Cinderella, there was Marilyn Monroe, along with prime-time regulars like Barbara Eden in *I Dream of Jeannie* and Jan Brady in *The Brady Bunch*. My desire for Happily Ever After did not wane; instead, it grew in leaps and bounds.

I had my first kiss in eighth grade and my first love in ninth, and what else was there to know? Who needed relationship skills when you had Erica Kane on *All My Children* and *General Hospital's* Luke and Laura for relationship coaches, Monday thru Friday? Everything you ever needed to know about relationships was right there, happening in reel time, reel life.

The first time my heart broke was when I watched my father drive away as I stood on our front lawn, paralyzed with agony, begging him at the top of my barely-eight-year-old lungs, "Please don't leave, Daddy! Oh Daddy, please don't leave!" Nothing could console me. I knew little of how to comfort myself after sustaining such a life-altering blow; nor did my mother. The only God I knew had just walked out the door. When he left, I felt as though the life was sucked right out of my body. My little spirit was shattered.

It took five seconds to break my heart the second time and approximately three days to swear to never, not ever again, be that vulnerable. Three entire days of being tortured by Technicolor reruns of me squirming on the ground, hanging onto my beloved's leg for dear life as he slid my fifteen-year-old body across the slick floor trying to escape my death grip, as I begged him not to leave me. He finally broke free, escaping with one less shoe, which I clutched in a fetal position, choking on mucus and tears, lying on the cold floor in a pathetic heap of annihilation.

Seventy-two hours of graphic recurrent thoughts of him having sex with not just the one other girl he was having sex with (aside from me), but *two* other girls—when he promised *me* his heart; said that he loved me, *only* me; that he wanted to marry me; that I was his soul mate, the only one for him, forever. That's 4,320 minutes of drowning in excruciating feelings of rejection, heart-wrenching abandonment, breathtaking insecurity and unrelenting blows of self-doubt. Or 259,200 seconds of scouring my mind for what was wrong with me, why he didn't want me, why I wasn't enough for him—punctuated by infinite nanoseconds of trying to console myself while figuring out how I could get him to love me again!

I decided that my father was right—all men wanted one thing. Aligning myself with this latest twist on my mythology—that men were pigs, not knights in shining armor, and that Cinderella was an idiot—I changed my role models. Simone de Beauvoir, Socrates and Edgar Cayce were my new heroes, tireless (and, well, dead) friends who would help to prepare me for the battle I would wage in the coming years. As predicted, all was fair in love and war!

HAPPILY EVER AFTER WHAT?

Our culture has been selling Happily Ever After for the past three hundred years. Julia Roberts plays a prostitute named Vivian in the film *Pretty Woman.* Richard Gere, playing a handsome and wealthy bachelor named Edward, becomes smitten with Vivian and offers her a real relationship with him. Later, as Vivian and her soon-to-be-ex roommate, Kit, sit poolside at the Beverly Wilshire, contemplating Vivian's revival, she says, "Come on, Kit, you and me live in the real world. Who gets to live Happily Ever After? Who?"

"Oh, the pressure of a name," replies Kit, rubbing her temples in an attempt to conjure a name for her curiously bereft pal. "I got it . . . Cinder-#&$@!ing-rella," she announces triumphantly. They both laugh at the absurdity and irony of her conclusion.

In her haste to accept her knight's proposal of Happily Ever After, Vivian fluffs her hair and looks at herself in the mirror, pronouncing, "Princess Vivian" and prepares to rescue him—the price she has set for her bail. But she doesn't realize it. Most of us don't. She'll deal with the consequences of whatever choices she makes . . . *later*. That's what we all tell ourselves. We don't ask what happens next, after we are rescued. Happily Ever After—WHAT? We watch the credits roll over our own lives, and surreptitiously delirious, amble along temporarily intoxicated on whatever fate will have for us.

Most of us pray hard that life will deal us a good hand; after all, we have been mostly good girls—except when we had no choice, we explain on bended knees. We did what "you" told us, we made every effort to smile even when we wanted to rip your face off, to be as pretty as possible despite our genetic inheritance.

We fluff our hair up and climb aboard the love boat too, because that's what Cinderella is supposed to do. Never mind that Prince Charming isn't actually that charming.

We don't stop to consider who we are with, instead of how they make us feel. We are so busy trying to fill the never-ending deficit of neediness that we haven't quite gotten around to the fact that who each of us is being speaks louder than words. We are too busy focusing on ending our pain and celebrating that someone wants us—that, perhaps, after all, we won't be alone, and just maybe we will live Happily Ever After. So, just like Vivian in *Pretty Woman*, we don't notice that our Edward

a) Has never been in a successful, healthy, mutually satisfying relationship.

b) Is emotionally unavailable, saying flat-out that fairy-tale relationships are too complicated.

c) Has little staying power when things don't go his way or someone expresses a legitimate need.

And, in Vivian's case, Edward thinks picking up a prostitute is a good idea.

It's a sleepy, almost drug-induced state in which we approach relationships: wanting or needing to get something. Our lack of foresight is due to the fact that most of us don't want to hear what the truth is, especially when it comes to relationships. We are addicted to the idea of Happily Ever After, and most of us aren't ready or willing to quit seeking the next high. Most of us are too busy bartering with God (or whatever your preference in terms is—The Divine, Nature, Jesus, Buddha, God, Allah, etc.), treading water with Mr. Right Now or trying to turn someone into "The One." The rest of us might be taking some down time in between rounds before we get back out there, baiting and mating, trying to catch and land the perfect partner—and of course live Happily Ever After—or at least better than last time!

There Is No Magic Love Potion

Most of us don't want to hear that relationships take work. We're not up for too much work; we are very busy people with lots on our plates! We don't want to hear that we need to love ourselves first, that we need to get clear on what we want, that we can't give what we don't have, and that water seeks its own level. Instead, we want to pick up some magical book or take "the" seminar or workshop that will change our lives miraculously with as little effort as possible. It has indeed become the American way—fast food, fast relationships. Everything has become equally disposable. What's more, we want, for our paltry investment, a very *high* return. It's not too much to ask, is it, to have true love, infinite abundance and to live Happily Ever After for all our *effort*? It's our birthright, some say—love, abundance and so on!

Well, if you are waiting for me to tell you there is a secret or a magic answer, I won't; because there isn't and that's the truth.

We don't want to hear that the answer to our suffering and pain is to love ourselves and take responsibility for our reality and experience. We are waiting (some of us secretly) to be swept away by our knight in shining armor. So we stay stuck, blaming everyone, everything—our childhood wounds, our circumstances. We choose to believe that life is unfair, or blame ourselves for not being enough. All the while, we perpetuate the belief that finding a great guy is a matter of manipulation or luck, that all relationships are hard and that men are dogs.

What I found, having believed all of the above myself (based on compelling evidence), is that I still longed for love, and found the only REAL way to create that for myself was to face the truth, that great relationships begin within. I had to study that concept and finally embody it. I know, firsthand, how hard it is to take responsibility for the course of *my* life, to look at how *I* created my experience, to understand the importance of forgiving my parents and myself—and ultimately, the struggle of truly learning how to love and honor myself. I always say my journey to living an impeccable life and staying the course (as much as I have been able to) is like trying to pull a 747 plane out of a nosedive. It takes everything you've got. But for me, at some point, the decision was easy—live free or die. I wanted the good stuff and was willing to do whatever it took to get it.

> *Great relationships begin within.*

By doing the work, no matter how hard or uncomfortable—shattering myth by myth, waking up from Happily-Ever-After denial by way of disenchantment—I finally found what I was looking for. As cliché as it sounds, it is a fact: True love is inside of me. It's simple as that. The best news of all is that, once found, no one can ever, ever take that away from me!

BLINDING HASTE AND
THE LIES WE TELL OURSELVES

After twenty-five years of being in the self-help industry (I started young), I want to bring the sacred back to sex and make self-love a household imperative, not an esoteric enigma or a cliché. I want to help you to celebrate yourself instead of selling yourself. I have figured out a way to do it by discovering what escapes so many of us: that when it comes to relationships, we need to slow . . . way . . . down. First we need to take care to know and love ourselves, know what we want in life and who we choose to be with. Having sex before we know ourselves seems to be the major culprit in heartbreak and the primary obstacle standing between our success and failure in relationships.

I witness it almost every day. Some woman, young or old, has again fallen bewitched by her need for love, not knowing what she needs or who she is—and next thing you know she is sharing her sacred self, her divine body, her most sacred life-force energy with another in the hopes that this time it will work out.

Not that sex is bad or wrong—heavens no! It's beautiful to express your love physically. However, most often it is when we share our bodies that we really fall, that expectations rise, that we start to see commitment ahead and are suddenly filled with needs and wants. We cross our fingers and plunge in, hoping that chemistry will be enough to keep him and we figure we will work out the rest later.

I have also noticed in my career that women are doing something we have never done before; we are starting *not* to care. The simple fact that we now can choose to freeze a guy's sperm in lieu of sacred union alarms me; what's more disturbing is that women are starting to behave like some men. We are starting to think that having sex is no big deal, that we can take a pill and Mother Nature won't mind, that having children is a novelty and raising them is a part-time *job* to be juggled along with the rest of life's trappings.

I believe we have stopped caring because we are becoming so out of touch with who we really are and our unique purpose in this life. We are starting to believe that being attractive is a value and that having sex is not a sacred act. That we must please others to be loved, that a man's penis can think, and that money alone actually makes us happy. And underneath it all, I am afraid that some of us honestly believe that death is preferable to a broken heart.

So, I devised six tools, which, when developed into skills, will help you navigate the otherwise unpredictable, yet ultimately quite predictable, course of your relationships. I can almost always tell at twenty paces which relationships will fail, primarily because neither person has developed these skills and is in a great hurry to quench their longing to be loved, rescued and saved from loneliness or hardship. And while the desire for coupling is primal, it is in our haste that we set ourselves up for heartache.

What You Will Get
from Reading This Book

I am well aware of our inclination to rationalize our choices. My own list has been very long and has included: *We learn from experience; I didn't have any good role models; I don't know anyone who is really happy; Relationships are hard; Better luck next time; I was just going through a phase; It was a rebound; We were too young; I didn't know any better; I had a crappy childhood; It was karma.*

The painful and disastrous relationship scenarios I have personally experienced and encountered with others over the years are staggering. They span betrayal and murder and everything in between. However, it was my awakening to the excruciating truth that love does not happen outside myself that prompted me to find a cure for my own suffering. And it is in sharing these stories that I hope you find yourselves and heed the following advice: The wise woman learns from her mistakes, the brilliant woman learns from other people's mistakes.

What I have to say to you seems to me gravely important, yet I know we each have our own journey to make. I hope that my experience and the stories of the other women that I am about to share will help summon the ineffable that promises to quench your heart's desire—to be in a healthy, loving relationship!

> *The wise woman learns from her mistakes, the brilliant woman learns from other people's mistakes.*
>
> 𝓶

I know men and women; I know what they want. I know when they are in lust and when they are in love, when they are lying and when they are telling the truth. I can usually tell by looking at someone what they are committed to, and in thirty seconds who they are pretending to be. For me these are not difficult assessments, rather a talent/gift that I have developed the hard way. These years of personal experience have helped make me an expert in my field. You need to be an expert in your own life, if you're not already—preferably without having to make the same mistakes, or without making the same mistakes *again*. It's not too late! Wherever you find yourself on your path, you have the opportunity to use your intuition and free will to develop these six tools. You don't have to become one of the 50 percent of all marriages that fail in divorce, to suffer from another broken heart, or worse, to sell your soul or lose your precious life.

I share all this because I want you to know that I understand. I know how incredibly painful, how utterly devastating, how excruciating it was for me to have my heart broken again and again—and then to swear, *never again*. And how, after using these tools I am about to share with you, I opened my heart again, which helped give me the strength and confidence I needed to create what I had always wanted—a healthy, fulfilling, sustainable relationship, starting with my relationship with myself.

I believe so many of us who choose this path of self realization, awakening and healing are like diamonds in the rough—a wealth of energy, passion, vitality and courage just waiting to be uncovered or discovered by our own selves. We have what it takes to heal and grow and, yes, care again. Deeply!

In the pages that follow, we will be discussing sex, love and chemistry, relationships, penises, broken hearts and death, not necessarily in that order.

I will share with you six stories about six women, as well as my own story: a single mom who keeps picking the same unavailable-but-fun, hunky guy again and again, who ends up paralyzed and in a wheelchair; a Ph.D. whose marriage was a twenty-six-year lie; a single thirty-something entrepreneur whose clock is ticking while she wonders why she can't find any good men "out there"; a young lady who just can't bring herself to ask her lover a few critical questions; a middle-aged divorcee who falls deeper into depression trying to free herself from an eight-year booty-call relationship; and a young woman who seemed to have it all— the perfect marriage, wealth, beauty, and after a decade of trying, twin girls—whose shocking story ends in homicide. I hope these stories will touch you, move you to be the best version of yourself, and inspire you to see that while learning from your mistakes is smart, learning from others' mistakes is #&$@!ing brilliant!

At the end of each story you will see what HINDSIGHT can be gained from these common, painful, heart-wrenching experiences, and you will be introduced to the corresponding tool for your relationship toolbelt. I have also included exercises to help you develop each tool into a skill that can and will serve you for the rest of your life—whether you are trying to find, get or keep a relationship.

We will explore in more depth specifically what I did to love myself, and how you can do it too. I will show you how to see exactly where you are focusing your attention, and how to create a self-inquiry practice so you have access to your highest truth twenty-four hours a day, seven days a week. You'll learn how to identify your own self-defeating patterns and stop repeating them; how to make a great list to help you attract a great relationship and then turn that list into a Self-Love Prescription. I give you fourteen questions you definitely want to ask a prospective partner before you rush into anything you'll be sorry for. I'll tell you the story about how I married myself—and how you can create a powerful commitment ceremony for yourself too! I will also share with you a ritual that helped me to let go of my past and a method for creating Consciousness Agreements that will give you the greatest opportunity for attracting and creating a healthy, fulfilling, sustainable relationship right now.

The tools and corresponding processes, exercises and rituals helped me create the life I live today and every day, the life of which I had only ever dreamed. I don't just teach this work, I live it! In hindsight, had I known *then* what I know today, I would have saved years of suffering.

This book will give you a foundation that will always support you in attracting and creating healthy, fulfilling, sustainable relationships. *Hindsight* offers you insights that you can use as foresight to protect yourself from immense, unnecessary struggle and heartache. *Hindsight* offers what you need to know *before* you drop your drawers.

All you have to do is *begin within*!

Chapter One

To Thine Own Self Be True

Your task is not to seek for love,
but merely to seek and find all the barriers
within yourself that you have built against it.
—RUMI

Here's the deal: if God had asked me, I would have made having a penis a privilege. A man would have had to go to school for years to earn the right to get one. Then he would be subjected to a battery of tests that he must pass, and *then* he'd stand before an all-woman council who would determine whether or not he met the necessary criteria to get one. And they'd then hand it over; "Here's your penis, sir, good luck with that." I know, bummer She didn't ask me.

In the meantime, I have spent twenty-five years of my adult life coming up with an alternative: the tools that are in this book. Since we have no control over the dispensing of men's penises, we do have control over the tools and skills *we have* before we encounter the penis ourselves!

Bringing the sacred back to sex, yourself and your life is the best investment you will ever make. Being true to yourself is where you must begin, even if you have to travel back in time to find where you left it. This book is about the journey of finding yourself again.

I was in the fifth grade, sitting on the floor underneath my desk, watching a filmstrip with the rest of my class one rainy afternoon. Unbeknownst to me, my girlfriends were conspiring to set me up with a boy that, up until that very afternoon, had made me gag. I'm not sure if he was *ugly*, per se, or if I was simply having trouble seeing past his favorite fare—his boogers—or his putrid stench: he smelled of farts and old socks. While the guiles of chemistry remained a mystery, it mattered little what this boy looked like; his character and habits screamed *ugly* to me (had he bathed, I might have felt different). Bottom line, he disgusted me. My friends, on the other hand, seemed to think we were a perfect match.

Apparently grime boy held a torch for me (in preadolescent dog years, this amounts to one week) and must have had an "in" with one of my tribeswomen, because next thing I knew I was being swarmed with enough peer pressure to consider anything—and anyway who could pass up all this attention at age ten? It wasn't every day you had the chance to become wildly popular, and I certainly wasn't immune to some *tween* paparazzi. Naturally, amidst all this fanfare and adoration, I said yes to this love-entranced, booger-eating, suitor's proposal—a soggy note he affectionately lobbed from across the floor, asking me to go steady with him.

I sat stunned, having sealed my fate as Mrs. Booger, my life flashing before my eyes. *Well, on the plus side, he seems to like me*, I thought. All other such weak, irrational drivel ended there.

Queen Maryanne, reluctant heir to Mr. Stinky's putrid throne. The more I thought, I thought *not*. There was nothing I could tell myself, as much as I loved being liked and wanted, to make me think this was a good idea. Besides, I could not escape the horrifying vision that he might want to touch me, or worse . . . kiss me! *But what if I hurt his feelings?* And again, the thought of disappointing my enthusiastic friends—oh, the pressure of the peers—temporarily paralyzed me with its horror.

Sir Stinky Booger gestured for me to come sit near him and watch the rest of the filmstrip—underneath a table in the dark; an obvious fate worse than death. The mere motion of his hand forced a terrible waft from clear across the room. The perceptible stench about knocked me out as I scrambled for pencil and paper and scribbled as fast yet as prettily as I could, "I am breaking up with you!" Then, I drew a heart (I suppose to soften the blow), added my name (made it seem more official), and had it couriered back to him forthwith. I sat in this hell, this prepubescent pit stop, for what seemed an eternity as I watched him unfold the note with what I could have sworn were hooves. Oddly, my feelings were mixed: my relief could not have been more palpable (unless, of course, someone had actually opened the door), while at the same time, I figured stinky people needed love too. But who said I had to be the sacrificial lamb? Even so, I figured he'd get over it even if he didn't get over me: a curious thought interrupted by yet another wadded paper that flew across the room, hitting his next victim in the head.

I sat on the floor with the slightest afterglow, ruminating on the rejection of my first semi-legitimate suitor, swirling the complexities like fine wine I had never before tasted, a subtle bouquet of victory and defeat. Not quite ripe from the experience, I was liberated at ten because I somehow knew I had been true to *myself*.

Well, I lost that youthful wisdom and confidence somewhere along the way.

THE MIRE

I once knew a young woman quite intimately who, like so many of us, had gotten deeply involved in a relationship backward, as it were. With a nine-month-old child, she was in the midst of a painful divorce, while trying to nurse a debilitating anxiety disorder. Instead of taking some time for herself to heal her wounds, let go of the past, reevaluate and get clear on what she wanted, commit to herself and follow her God-given intuition for guidance—she shut down. This made her feel even more lost and alone. She decided that unless she hurried, she would miss her chance at Happily Ever After, which was all she had ever wanted to be. So, she leaped into the arms of the first acceptable suitor that came courting. The fact that he was her boss made things difficult. The fact that he was married made them worse.

Their chemistry was unrivaled, an obvious sign they belonged together. A year or so later, both divorced, they decided to make a go at a serious relationship. In the beginning they found great comfort as friends, each offering what the other seemed to lack—he security, she understanding. Until, that is, the scales began to tip and the truth of what lay underneath it all began to slowly and painfully reveal itself. They became casualties, broken and harmed by each other's unwillingness to recognize and accept their own mistakes (one of which was the mistaken belief that chemistry is love). The very same thing that brought them together—she was frightened and he was unhappy—would rip them apart precious years later. Several police reports would stain his record, her heart and their relationship, forever. Sounds a bit like the back cover jacket to a sordid romance novel, doesn't it? Unfortunately, it wasn't fiction.

"Don't you dare mistake my vulnerability for weakness, you son of a bitch," she said, holding her face, trying to hold back her tears.

"Get out!" he shouted, slamming on the brakes and pulling the car to the side of the road. "Just get out of the #&$@! car!"

"What are you talking about?" She panicked. "You want *me* to get out?" Her heart was pounding. She was having an anxiety attack, which changed everything; now she was trapped between fighting for self-respect and fighting for her life. "You're not going to drop me in the middle of nowhere, in the rain . . . at night. You're ridiculous!"

He hated when she belittled him; it only pissed him off more. Grumbling under his breath, he impulsively pulled the car away from the curb and back down the road. She barely allowed herself to feel great relief that he had reconsidered dumping her out, temporarily taking the edge off of her biggest fear—being abandoned. "What did you just say?" she asked indignantly.

"You heard me," he said.

"No, I did not," she challenged him.

"You wanted it."

She turned her head. "I wanted . . . what?"

"You wanted that guy's attention."

"You just punched me in the face . . . because I wanted it?"

"I just hit you back after you slapped me."

"You called me a . . . cunt! Who says that? It's the most . . . arghhh . . . I can't believe . . ." Her words trailed off and her face, still throbbing from the blow, streamed with tears. Unable to make sense of his bizarre behavior, terrified he would drop her in the middle of the night, she sensed quickly that she was not in the power position, not safe.

As she would tell it, they were at a wedding, sitting at the reception table. A guest asked her to dance, even though she was obviously unavailable. Shortly, her boyfriend got up to use the bathroom, leaving her alone. The guest approached her again, this time remarking, "Who's that loser, and why would you be with him when you could be with me?"

She said it was her boyfriend and she'd take him any day over this wanker, however good-looking or charming. Her boyfriend returned and they left shortly thereafter. The only mistake she made that night, the way she saw it, was telling him what the wanker had said—which she professed she did out of loyalty. I suspect this was a partial truth; the greater truth was, she wanted him to know that she was desired by other men, perhaps making him jealous and reminding him what a great catch she was. Her insecurity backfired, big time.

The way he saw it was simple: she was a whore, flirting unabashedly with strangers, leaking her sexuality for everyone to see, embarrassing him and making him look like a fool. Therefore, she had asked for it, punch and all.

"It's over," he declared.

She knew he was serious. "It's over?" She was thinking he should be *apologizing* to her, begging her for forgiveness, not dispassionately tossing her to the curb like an old newspaper. The searing pain of his indifference, followed by this ultimate blow came tumbling down on her. "It's okay. Let just pretend it never happened, okay? Please, come on . . . let's not do this . . . we have been through so much . . . don't do this." She was surprised by the words spilling out of her mouth. And then she said it, breaking into a million pieces. "I love you . . ." breaking her own heart, abandoning herself in the midst.

He followed her inside, which to her meant that perhaps he was reconsidering the breakup. The power pendulum was swinging toward what she considered her favor. This wasn't the first time they had split. Theirs had been a relationship built on passion and little rationale. He had been rough with her before, but he had never thrown an actual punch.

"Oh my God!" she shrieked, running out from the bathroom and down the hall to her bedroom, where he had settled, trying to shrug off the night. She lunged at him. He grabbed both of her arms midair and caught her wild swing just before one of her fists landed in his face.

"Are you insane?" he shouted at her, bending her this way and that, trying hard to contain her rage.

"Look at my face!" she screeched. "I have a black eye . . . oh my God! Now what am I going to do? I have a shoot to do tomorrow. I can't do it now!" she wailed. She was scheduled to start shooting a television pilot barely eighteen hours later.

Filled with renewed fury, she flailed her arms again, wriggling loose from his straitjacket grip and pounding on his chest. "You piece of #&$@!, I can't believe you did this to me, and . . . you didn't even say you were sor—"

She was crying so hard she couldn't finish her sentence. Because she knew he wasn't . . . sorry. What he was now was furious. He just wanted to get away from her, so he took off for the front door. She, of course, ran after him, stumbling and falling over the high heels that she kicked off when they had arrived.

"Don't leave!" she shouted. Picking herself up, she scuffled to the door and watched him pile himself into his car. "You coward . . . you ASSHOLE!" she screamed at the top of her lungs, for the whole neighborhood to hear. "Go ahead and run, you big pansy!"

Her tirade ended as soon as she heard the click of his car door unlocking. He emerged like a titan, fixed on shutting her up—perhaps permanently, she guessed by the look on his face. She did a one-eighty and hightailed it back inside, locking the front door behind her, but he raced around back and came through the bedroom French doors. He grabbed her around the waist, covering her mouth with his hand. She kicked and punched and finally got hold of some skin, and bit him so hard he dropped her. Before she could get up, he had her again. This time he was unable to shut her up, and she was unable to stop the emasculating windfall of obscenities. He lost all control and threw her against the wall. She splatted like a fly smacked against a windshield on the freeway, and slid down, suddenly realizing she couldn't feel her legs. Unable to move, in a great deal of shock, she decided to just stay quiet. He caught his breath and waited to see what she was going to do next.

"I . . . can't feel my body," she said after a few more minutes passed, unable to look him in the face. He didn't speak. They sat together, shaken and exhausted.

She thought about how this was different from the time he had waited in her backyard, shrouded in a blanket, and burst into her house in a jealous rage to beat up a male friend who she had gone to the movies with. Never mind that they had technically broken up. And it was different from the time he had tied her up with a telephone cord so she wouldn't leave because he had lost control after an argument—again. The difference was palpable. She could taste the blood in her mouth from the impact.

Make no mistake, she was no angel here. She had fought back, started fights, goaded him on in her own blindness. She was still convinced that she had the power to make him be who she needed him to be.

Sure, she made resolutions to stay away, sought counsel from friends who implored her to end it, sustained threats of him being banished from her family. She even lost one of her closest and dearest true friends because this friend was unable to continually bear witness to such blatant, horrific displays of low self-esteem and abuse. This time would be different, she told herself. This time she would teach him a lesson that would fix everything.

They spent the next few weeks apart, relieved to have the break. Yet, her resentment and rage grew. She had gone to great lengths and sacrificed much for this relationship, and as a testament of her devotion now attended a weekend relationship workshop with him, hoping that they could find some way to resolve the ever-widening gap between them. They truly were a demonstration of the expression, "You can't live with 'em, you can't live without 'em." Soon they were, how you say, back in the saddle again.

"Sex for sex's sake," he was saying to a friend on the phone, pontificating on what he had gleaned from the workshop. It was enough to make her sick. Never mind that he had yet to apologize for the latest round of their clash of ills and wills, his obsession with sex was wearing on her. Being curious and experimenting was one thing, being dependent on it was another. Now he had somehow managed to take the wisdom this couple had shared with them in their beautifully orchestrated workshop and boil it down to having "sex for sex's sake." This was the last straw. She had been feeling like she needed to take a break from all his fantasies and storytelling and pornographic preoccupation. She just felt tired—and, well, dirty—and, ironically, was about to propose that they learn to be intimate in other ways so they could strengthen their relationship. This was a sincere effort on her part to find her center of self-respect and self-love. She deluded herself into thinking he would understand when she would explain how important it was for her to be chaste for the sake of her own healing.

"Are you telling me you will leave me if I don't have sex with you?"

she repeated, naively. She stood up, put her hands on her hips, took a step back and stared him dead in the eyes.

"That's right, having sex with you is too important for me," he said unflinchingly.

"Look, it's important to me that I know you love me…you know, *for me* and not just because I turn you on or whatever," she said earnestly, feeling awkward and quite vulnerable. She had never before even considered saying no to sex.

She was on the brink of liberation, or so she hoped.

"I don't see what the point is. Having sex for sex's sake is what they said would bring us closer," he said.

"I think they say that because most people don't have sex three or four times a day for what, four years in a row now, like we do. Most people probably have sex way less," she said, not knowing how to defend her deepest urge to abstain for a while. "I can't explain it," she started.

"That's because it doesn't make sense," he said, biting at one of his fingernails and beginning to lose interest. Incensed, she turned around and huffed out of the room, secretly devastated. She could not face the glaring truth, though he had just thrust it in her face.

He was about as deep as paint and she was too wounded to be anyone's partner without attending to her past hurts and wounds. She had made her best effort, she thought, to stand up for herself, to speak up about her needs. But she surrendered to what seemed like the truth—that until *he* would change, they would never have a chance. Until *he* would get ahold of his out-of-control sexual appetite, she would never feel secure. Until he would love her *and only her*, she would always be insecure. He assured her there was no chance in hell he was ever going to change and that she should simply be happy with her life. At this point, she was not willing to share her life with him any longer. He could not honor her needs and she was unwilling to stay unless he did. She was a far cry from fifth grade as she lay in bed these many years later.

She continued to let that lie dictate her reality—that "Until *men* change, we cannot truly have a chance at love and feel secure. We should face facts. That's just the way it is, the way men are, and we should do as we are told—be happy." But she could not. I remember it so clearly, because "she" was me!

Years passed, as well as several different relationships that continued to trample my liberation along with any self-worth and self-esteem I may have tasted early on. I now fostered the popular belief that I didn't exist unless someone loved me, and that Happily Ever After was the only dream worth pursuing. There I was, with every blessing in the world—skinny, tan, and rich—yet soul-sick and suffering, at the precipice of a revelation that would forever change my life.

Having made every effort to be lovable and to find the one who would rescue me from myself—with no real sense of who I was, and a long, long way from that day in fifth grade when I was true to myself—I found myself helpless and hopeless. Quite honestly, I was tired of surviving. I clearly didn't know how to live, and felt like I couldn't go on.

HINDSIGHT: GREAT RELATIONSHIPS BEGIN WITHIN

I wasn't always color blind, unable to see red flags; nor was I always so externally referenced, believing love would make me whole. As you saw earlier, I started out like most of us, with a fully intact spirit and flawless intuition that I naturally relied upon. I had an authentic freedom of being that translated to me ultimately being true to myself.

But just like the Julia Roberts character, Vivian, says in *Pretty Woman*, "People tell you enough bad things about yourself, and after a while you start to believe it!"

I love what Maryanne Williamson said so beautifully in her book *A Return to Love*: "Our deepest fear is not that we are inadequate. Our deepest fear is that we are powerful beyond measure."

It was easier for me to believe I was flawed and unlovable, because I was tired—tired of being put down and beat up, and afraid of being alone. I started to see that maybe my father was right. Because I believed him and them and whatever self-sabotaging headline my mind had the habit of telling me, I compromised my spirit, my body and my soul. I could no longer hear what my heart truly longed for. I became numb from the head down! I had managed to achieve success on the outside—I had the man, the home, the family, the body, the clothes and the jewelry. I had an immense psychological arsenal; by the time I was twenty-one I had read hundreds of books ranging from Kierkegaard to Swedenborg, Simone De Beauvoir to Socrates, Krishnamurti to Cayce, the Bible to Shakti Gawain, and I fancied myself mentally agile enough to run philosophical circles around most people. What I did not know yet, what I didn't have, was myself.

It wasn't as though I was asleep throughout my prior relationships—heavens, no! I would wake up and then fall back to sleep. I could hear my intuition and take a stand, but fall back to sleep because I had not developed an internal sense of myself that was strong enough not to get trampled by another's opinions or the recurrent loop of my old, deeply ingrained, patterns of self-sabotage, abuse and wounds. I did not yet have the Daily Practice I share with you in chapter 3 and I still believed I was unable to change *them*. I had yet to make the unfathomable leap from being externally referenced to being internally referenced. Only after I learned to love myself, to celebrate and commit to myself, to get clear on what I wanted for myself and in a relationship, to resurrect my intuition and lead with it instead of my sexuality, to develop my discernment and learn how to interview well and communicate responsibly—only then did I manage to attract and create a healthy, fulfilling sustainable relationship.

I kept at it, I kept reading and studying and learning enough to hang onto the belief that there was another way—until I collapsed and woke up, realizing the other way was to *begin within*!

Chapter Two

Skinny, Tan and Rich, and Then I Woke Up

Don't forget to love yourself.
—SOREN KIERKEGAARD

One day I awakened slowly, feeling tired and heavy. I wanted to pull the covers back over my head and disappear under my expensive, tasteful duvet. Instead, I flung out of bed and headed for my tennis shoes. While I made and drank a cup of herb tea (no sugar, no milk), I fantasized about eating at least three of my son's Eggo waffles piled high, separated by obscene mounds of butter, glistening with just enough maple syrup not to drown in.

Looking at myself in the mirror as I brushed my teeth with whitening paste (never wondering how white was white enough), I noticed I felt plain. So, after I washed, toned, moisturized and sun-blocked, I promptly applied liner and lipstick—careful not to exaggerate the actual fullness of my lips, even though big, fat, fake lips were becoming in vogue. I gave myself a second examination, face approximately one centimeter from the mirror, bobbing in and away, assessing all possible vantage points ritualistically. Then I realized that my rear end had not yet been checked for clearance. My eyes softened reflexively from wide-screen to half-mast; I unconsciously longed for good news, but prepared for the harsh reality. How big was too big? Considering my unforgiving palate for perfection, there was little wiggle room where my ass was concerned.

I had spent considerable amounts of time and energy to minimize my maximus and even more time trying to camouflage it. How I had it: Big ass equals bad day. On this day, however, I maintained acceptable girth, harmonized with successful camouflage. *Ass check complete; ready for lift-off. Wait. Nice ass is great, but wealthy nice ass is a rare commodity, which equals higher incidence of self-esteem. Must add giant diamond ring. Ahhhh, yes . . . there we go. I am obviously worth something. Much better!*

True, it had become common to see huge diamond earrings, visible at twenty paces, injected in earlobes across the country. They were easy to come by—all us Happily-Ever-After-addict chicks had access to fakes that looked real. But who had anything real anymore? Particularly, real bling? I did, and that made me feel special, not to mention less fat, unworthy and ugly—which worked for me. At least, temporarily . . .

Did I mention I had gotten engaged? I tried not to think about that; it brought up "bed" and, well, sex, which over the years had become a painful and heartbreaking topic. At this point there were very few safe zones in my life and, generally speaking, bed had never been one of them. I was aware of the haunting aphorism, "Wherever I go, there I am," and there were not many places left to hide. Try as I might to haggle with reality, my hungers, reflections, feelings, failures, hopes and desires were crackling and ripping through me like a thunderstorm brewing. I spent the rest of that morning counting . . . one alligator, two alligators.

"Excuse me . . . I think I am first here—unless 'car on right goes first' is beyond your scope of understanding!" I yelled, as I fled from one stop sign to a screeching halt at the next one. I didn't dare drink caffeine, but if you didn't know me, you'd have bet that this car jockey had dosed up on it.

"Ohh Jeeezusssssss," I hissed, spying the line at Longs' checkout counter. *Who comes here at 8:30 A.M.? I mean, what couldn't wait, for God's sake?* If I had stood any nearer to the little old woman in front of me, I could have given you her hair follicle count. I think she could feel my breath on her head. She turned around cautiously and looked up into my face—the face of a toothy (very white, of course), salivating, flesh-eating beast with a supernatural, top-of-the-food-chain look on its face. The old woman crept forward, making no sudden moves, so I wouldn't rip her head off her shoulders. *Good idea, Grandma*, I thought. *Keep it moving, people, because in about two seconds you're all going down like bowling pins.*

Just then the cashier thought we all might be better served if she took an extra few minutes to finish up a price check while simultaneously attempting to fill out a return slip—for her first time! *Great idea!* I thought, as my blood began to thicken and boil. *Super.* Now the man in front of Grandma was pulling at his collar, maybe because I was sharing my usually private profanities with my new friends.

"UN#&$@!BELIEVABLE! Really, un#&$@!believable!" I declared. "Hey, maybe we should head over to aisle twelve and bust out some camping equipment. Surely none of us have anything better to do, eh?" I announced, speaking deliberately and directly to everyone in my immediate proximity.

The space between the rest of the line and me grew wider as my volume increased. "Oh, are we moving? That's fantastic. It's a miracle!" My sarcasm had invisible arms and legs challenging anyone, including small children and animals, to a duel. I knew that what was coming next had to be on par with a sonic explosion of major proportions. I was right at the brink of losing it, for real. I could not bear one more fake smile, one more agreeable word or nod. I could not pretend I didn't care how people looked at me. I could not stuff another feeling. I could not withstand one more ounce of judgment, yours or mine. I could not fake one more orgasm. I could not stand, for one more moment, this silent scream that felt like it would kill me if I did not let it out. But where? At *Longs*? How could I? I suddenly realized that what had overgrown inside of me was too big and too loud, not to mention too insane, to let loose in public. My mind raced. I panicked.

I had totally lost sight of the fact that I had come to Longs to purchase tennis balls that I didn't even need. I had no match. I was late for nothing. There was nowhere I needed to be. Where was I going? And why was I trying to get there so fast that I entertained homicidal thoughts? *OMG, I'm insane. I can't stop—I'd better get out of here!* Then I heard that still, small voice that I heard from time to time—one that I was sure was from a source greater than myself, because it spoke to me about things that were profound, rarely about things I wanted to hear: *Perhaps you are not trying to get **to somewhere**, Maryanne. Perhaps you are trying **to get away from yourself**.*

"Uhhhggghhhhh," I groaned as I heard this truth resound in my body. The clerk, with raised eyebrows, handed me my bag, as if she were hoping I wasn't far from whatever medication I needed. I couldn't have cared less. The sentence was repeating itself like it might do in a fun house; but this was not fun, and going mad was not really on the menu.

I dove into my car and ripped out of the parking lot, going in no particular direction. I wondered, as I sped through town, if I could park my car up in the hills somewhere and scream. You know the kind of scream I mean? The bloodcurdling kind that is bigger than me, louder than sound, loud enough that dogs around the world can hear it. The kind of scream that I never dared make—it was far too frightening, and the hallmark of people who actually are crazy. But it had to come out, whatever was in me. I knew I couldn't do it on the freeway because someone would see me. *What about the hill above my house? But what if someone heard me?* Where was far enough from civilization that I could let out this beast, but not so far that if it ripped me open I couldn't get help?

Trapped. The realization sunk in—there was nowhere I could feel all the way out loud. My jailbreak was a false alarm. I ended up driving home and flinging myself on my bed, managing somehow to choke back the inevitable. Yet, for some reason, on this particular day the heaviness of my sentence—housing this silent scream—became so unbearable that I could not escape the truth of it. I had tried everything I knew to be happy, to find Happily Ever After. I was thirty-something, I had survived three alcoholics, one drug fiend and another who stuck a loaded gun in my mouth. I had been proposed to at least a dozen times and married seven less than Elizabeth Taylor, and had developed a debilitating panic disorder that I would fight and suffer with for the next decade. A long way from Cartoon Town, indeed.

Unhappy, exhausted and paralyzed with fear, I grasped at everything and anything to ease my suffering. I knew that the problem was "something is wrong with me—and you, of course—and if we were just more (fill in the blank) everything would be okay." (In hindsight, I had the first part half right.)

My obsession with self-help began. I left no modality unturned. I tried twelve-step programs, psychiatrists, psychotherapists, hypnotherapists. I read well over a thousand self-help books and fell deeply in like with consulting unseen forces. I listened to astrologers, astrocartographers, numerologists, psychics, shamans, tarot readers, palm readers and people who were certain I was from another planet—which at the time seemed like a possibility (and a relief).

In addition to the psycho-spiritual realm, I tried other remedies. I left the country, changed my hair color, practiced Tantra yoga; tried pole dancing, role playing, speaking with different accents. I took up mountain-bike riding, tried to like pornography and playing golf; attempted to enjoy giving oral sex, drank more, stopped drinking, ate more and less, had an abortion, had a baby, became a counselor, wrote angry letters, filed several police reports, opened my third eye and finally . . . turned a blind eye. After all that research and development, rather than being an authority on anything—particularly on love, sex and relationships—I still felt desperate and alone.

Precious years passed. I often lay alone next to someone I *loved* but didn't *like*, comforted and repulsed by his physical presence, feeling, and believing I was wasting my life, plagued by insecurity and anxiety. I was sleeping with the enemy, or so it seemed. I thought love was passion, something worth fighting for, something that if you're lucky, happens once in your life, that makes you sick in its absence, jealous in its presence, violent when threatened and makes you want to die when it's gone. Hearing the words, "I've never felt this way before, I miss you, I love you, I can't have you be with anyone else" had been my reason to live.

Desperate for these words, I was accomplice to ongoing stories of cruelty and deceit: *It wasn't me; I didn't sleep with her; You are the only one; I never loved my wife; I want to marry you.* All this was punctuated by five police reports, three alcoholics, one drug dealer, and a sex fiend—the price I paid for *love.*

Now, lost and alone, I lay desecrated, sprawled across my bed like dead weight, ready to die, letting go of any hope I had left of finding love or what was wrong with me (and you) and fixing it so I could love and be loved and live Happily Ever After. My wracked body and exhausted, emaciated spirit were spent; reliving, recycling the same relationship story over and over, the rest of my life was only the backdrop. Same old story. I always chose someone whom I had to convince that I was worthy of being loved, someone who needed a lot of fixing, someone who had some major addiction, someone who did not see or "get" me. All of them made me feel bad about myself, or worse than I already did. All of them brought out the worst in me. Each relationship ended up the same . . . over.

I did not have the courage or the energy to kill myself. At this point, I didn't have the energy even to try. All I could do was lie there in the deafening silence. My body lay numb atop my covers while minutes turned to hours. The sun cast shadows that slithered across my bedroom walls. I didn't wonder if I was depressed: I had always been too spastic and anxious to allow myself the luxury of indulging the time that depression seemed to demand. I didn't wonder if I was drooling on my expensive bedspread, I didn't care if my mascara bled all over the 800-thread-count sheets. I didn't care that the phone rang and rang. I didn't even notice that I didn't care. I was just blank, zip, gone for real into another zone.

Some time later that afternoon, in this state of expanded nothingness, I stumbled into the bathroom and watched the tears drip from my nose. The only part of me that was real barely squeaked out the words, "God, help me. Are you there? Please, if someone is there . . . somewhere . . . anywhere . . . please talk to me. I'm sorry. I failed. If you're not there . . . I can't do this anymore!"

My whole body wailed. I couldn't stand up, so I stumbled back to bed and my prayer emerged; the first real prayer I may have ever prayed as an adult. One where I didn't need to get out of a jam, I wasn't calling in any favors, I wasn't bargaining or trying to beg life to rearrange itself for me—again. It wasn't the "no shame, no gain" plan. Nope, just one simple prayer. I slid off the side of my bed onto my knees, buried my face into my prayer-shaped hands, and said, "Please, if you're out there, *show me* the way . . . "

What happened next was the beginning of a life beyond my greatest imagination. In that next moment, I knew I was "home," I was full. No gaping hole. No missing parts. Everything suddenly appeared as it should be—whole and complete. I was not *at* peace; I *was* peace. I didn't know how it happened; I just knew everything was finally okay. I was okay inside and out. I had been given grace, and the gift of seeing myself as though for the very first time. The pain was simply, suddenly gone. I couldn't explain it, and I was afraid to question it. I had spent my whole life trying to get somewhere, away from somewhere else, away from whomever I believed I was, trying to be someone else, and the chasm seemed impossible to bridge! I wanted to stop hurting, suffering and dying inside, trying desperately to find Happily Ever After.

Having tried every way I knew, I finally gave up, exhausted and defeated. I surrendered at last and, miraculously, found myself on the other side. I had "died" and awakened in Happily Ever After. Only instead of it being some place *out* there, Happily Ever After had been there all along—deep inside of me.

Weeks passed and I still had a smile smeared across my face, as though I had just fallen in love. (Mostly, people thought I was high.) I had fallen in love, all right: I had fallen in love, Happily Ever After, with my precious, sacred self.

Everything seemed surreal, extra beautiful, stunning and vivid—downright dreamy. Nothing mattered and everything was deeply meaningful. My overall pace had dropped to about five miles per hour, which was a radical departure from my usual eighty-miles-per-hour-in-a-school-zone. This new reality made driving my car, for example, an interesting challenge. Almost everything suddenly fascinated me in a childish kind of way—the shiny knobs, the sky, the fact that I *could* drive, wondering where everyone was going. It kept fascinating me to the point where I would forget why I had gotten in the car.

Everyone else had plenty to say about my new whereabouts in the woo-woo-hippie zone.

"Mommy, are you okay? You're acting weird," said my six-year-old son, Warren. He was apparently concerned about my complete preoccupation with a housefly that had, curiously to me, circuitously landed on the kitchen windowsill.

"Maybe Heath should drive me to school?" he said in his wise little manner.

"Look at your face . . ." I gushed, "it's soooo gorgeous!" I careened, grabbing at his cheeks, forgetting all about the fly.

"Mahhhhm, stop!" He pleaded. But he couldn't help laughing a little because I was making a scrunchy face and laughing so contagiously.

It did not occur to me that I was being any "way," weird or otherwise. I was just happy, for no reason; it was a kind of bliss that happened from *inside* of me instead of from without. All my thoughts and feelings, all those voices that had chattered for so many years—everything was at once in harmony. Simply put, I stopped hurting, my longtime suffering was over, and I knew that I was free. My heart had opened after years of closing down. I knew I had crossed a threshold.

That day on my bed, alone and wishing I could die, I had no idea how close I was to being right—that love *was* the answer and that I had been missing the relationship of my dreams. I just didn't know that the person who would love me so deeply would turn out to be me.

HINDSIGHT:
IT STARTS WITH HOW WE TREAT OURSELVES

While it's true I had been beaten up, raped and abused, it is *how poorly I treated myself* that has prompted me to write this book. And, though many years have passed since that time and my life now is filled with all that I had then only ever dreamed of, I am compelled again and again to offer what I found that changed my life so profoundly—the priceless hindsight, the absence of which almost cost me my life.

I had come up with many anecdotes for my pain and its causes over the years, most of which seemed seated in the belief that a great relationship was what would ultimately make me happy. I tried to be prettier, thinner, sexier, less jealous, more—or less—confident in myself; I tried to care more, to care less, and finally not to care at all.

When I started looking in the Mirror—really, honestly looking at me, at who I really was and was not—I realized these men were not to blame for my misery, however heartily they participated in it. They were simply a perfect reflection of how I felt about myself, of who I was being and where I was at that time of my life. They reflected what I most valued, and didn't, about myself. They simply behaved in accordance with my highest truth about myself. Nor were my parents to blame, however heavy their hands; they simply taught me what they knew, laid the tracks, reflecting their own selves, values and experiences in life onto me.

My awakening introduced me more deeply to an ongoing process of self-inquiry, a practice of self-care and love. My lifelong practice of looking *outside* of myself for answers turned to looking *inside*. This great act of self-love unalterably changed my life more profoundly than almost anything I had ever done.

Yes, I had heard over the years, "You need to love yourself," "You can't give what you don't have," etc., so much so that it had become cliché. I considered myself a unique case, far too complicated for such simplistic ideas. Never mind the thought of spending precious time doing God-knows-what in the name of loving myself, which seemed suspiciously self-centered and, given my history, wasn't advisable. These are only some of the rationalizations and lies I told myself.

If it hadn't taken me thirty-three years to figure this all out, I might be shopping right now instead of trying to concoct for you an *anti-venom* for such fairy tales. A substantial dose of truth, one heart filled with compassion, a dose of hindsight and a swift kick in the pants ought to be the perfect drip for mainlining reality, chased with disenchantment.

I pause to look upon a lifetime of experimentation, impressed that I did not die from my vigilant pursuit of Happily Ever After. I wonder, as I sit here after all these years, if it's too good to be true that I have found what I sought for so long. I still have to pinch myself sometimes. The road from heartbreak to happiness has been worth every ounce of effort; it is not merely a dream, not a fairy tale, but a real-life love story. I had searched everywhere else and, finally, gratefully, fumbled upon the one thing I had not really embraced or explored fully—essentially, loving myself. I had been blessed with the gift of knowing what was possible, but I also knew that this feeling, this knowing, could not be maintained unless I chose to think differently, respond differently and do things differently. The tools I share throughout this book will help you to do the same.

Chapter Three

Don't Just Talk About It, SHOMI®

Everyone has created an image of himself.
That image is false, but we cling to the image and
this clinging becomes the barrier toward moving within.
—OSHO

In the chapters that follow, I will be introducing you to the things you need to know before you drop your drawers, and the things you need to do in order to maintain your sense of self while in relationship with another. I have learned that having a Daily Practice is a powerful way of creating and maintaining a constant stream of health, happiness and self-esteem. Prior to this discovery, I had become accustomed to bits of enlightenment followed by suffering and despair. It was like I would wake up and then go back to sleep, sometimes for embarrassingly long periods of time! I would read a book or find some great advice or go to a workshop; and then two months, two weeks or even two minutes later, fall back asleep, wondering where all that wisdom went (out the window again).

So, out of necessity, I created a way to help me stay awake to my inner source of love and fulfillment. A practice became the foundation for creating the healthy, fulfilling, loving relationship I have today. It all started with healing my relationship with myself, and having this practice will help you too.

A practice, preferably a *Daily* Practice, will provide the opportunity for you to not just "know the tools" but to transform them into skills that will serve you eternally. The Daily Practice is an invitation to truly give yourself some time each day to do the personal work needed to master this material. More importantly, the Daily Practice will give you the time to get to know yourself.

You can't get where you want to go without the ability to assess where you are in any given moment. A personal practice will serve that purpose. If healthy, loving relationships are what you seek, this is truly where to start. As I have said before, and I will say again, great relationships begin within. The method I'm about to share with you is the way within.

Having a daily spiritual practice, in and of itself, is foreign to most of us, except when we are experiencing discomfort or some kind of obvious crisis. Only then do we stop, inquire and ask for help or guidance. We wake up for a while to the reality that there is a bigger picture out there, that we have direct access to wisdom, guidance and help. Then, as soon as the discomfort or crisis has passed, we carry on. Many of us go back to sleep and rarely look back. So it would be safe to say we have a periodic practice, one of crisis or malady.

The invitation here is to embrace your life in a greater context, one that is supported by self-inquiry. A practice of looking for, and regularly seeking, the truth, which will ultimately give you the ability to live the life you truly desire—full of freedom of being. A life where being fake is no longer a reflex you need to survive. A life of self-love and self-respect. A life where peace and ease are a real part of your existence. A life filled with choices. A life met with curiosity and wonder. The life that you really want to live.

The catch is you must do the work. Period. No one, and I mean no one, is immune from this reality. If you want freedom, you must do the work. If you want peace, you must feel the old pain. If you want self-love, you must face what's most fake and ugly about yourself and others. It is my experience that if we want a great quality of life and to experience real freedom of being, we need to *practice daily*. You must face yourself and do what's necessary. You must seek the truth.

Why do the work? This, my friend, is your life. The only one you have. As my dear friend always says, "You might as well be yourself; everyone else is taken!" Here would be a good place to decide how much effort you are worth. How much time, how much energy, are you willing to give yourself, to get what you have been seeking for so long?

Don't worry if discipline is difficult, as it is for most of us. That's why it's called a *practice*. You don't have to be perfect. A practice is meant to help you wake back up and remember what you are working toward.

SHOW ME THE WAY

Let me introduce you to the SHOMI® method of body-centered self-inquiry. This process was named after the prayer I spoke the day I hoped that God would just beam me up and take me away from my pain and suffering. I said, "If you're out there, God, please *show me* the way!" And He did! The SHOMI philosophy is, "Your mind is here to serve your body, so you can follow your spirit." All the wisdom you will ever need about yourself is available to you any time, right there inside your body. All you need to do is learn how to listen to it and then trust its guidance.

How you start is simple:

Pick a time, it does not matter when. If you are a morning person, do it then. If you are a night person, start doing it then. If you are neither, just make sure you do it.

And sit down. That's right, sit down with yourself. Okay, fine, stand, lie down, whatever. Don't go to sleep or space out, though—you actually want to *be with yourself*. Yes, this is a concept that seems fairly unattractive for many of us at first, because there might be a lot of yuck in there that we only feel when we are quiet with ourselves. Trust me, you'll get past that eventually. The truth is that the "yuck" is there whether we take the time to notice it or not. When we don't pay attention to it, it finds a way to sabotage us. By taking the time to attend to it, we can either lessen its impact or release it completely.

In the meantime, it's worth saying for those who are literal, like me, and need clear instructions: No books, no words, no distractions, no music. This is a process of being with yourself so you can get to know yourself, so you can learn to care for yourself. Learn to listen to yourself, so you can learn to heal yourself, so you can learn to love yourself. Only then will life reflect all that beauty to you. 'Cause for now, life treats you the way you treat yourself. I'll share more on this later, but for now, take a look at your life.

> *Life treats you the way you treat yourself.*
>
> ℳ

If you ignore yourself, so does life. If you don't care for yourself, neither does life. And if anyone says they care for you, if you're abusing and neglecting yourself, you simply won't believe them anyway and are likely to do something to sabotage the relationship to prove yourself right. It's a physics law—NO two things can occupy the same place at the same time. You cannot have two conflicting beliefs about yourself without having psychic schism. Okay, in other words, it will make you crazy!

The good news is that a system—the human being is a system; mind, body, spirit—reorganizes itself to the highest available truth. That means, if you break through to the real truths about yourself and change the old ones, your whole world will realign. For example, when you switch the belief from "I am not enough" to "I *am* enough," your life will change, as will the world around you. Yes, this takes doing some work, and it takes discipline—lots, probably. It did for me, and aren't you worth it? Hey, it beats the alternative; more of the same old, same old.

So sit down, be quiet and ask, *What's here?* Or, as I like to ask, *What do I need to know right now?* And then listen. Pay attention.

Miraculously, your body will tell you. You may take a while to get the hang of it, but I promise, your body will speak to you. That does not mean you will like what it says. Oftentimes we have neglected ourselves and the body is NOT happy. Whatever the case, pay attention. Ask, *What do I notice about myself?* or *Show me what I need to know?* Then just listen. Yep, that's all. But to truly make it a practice versus a one-time experience, you will need to do it regularly.

Trust me when I tell you it's *foolproof.* Thank God, in my case, because the first year or so after I started this practice of listening to my body and its accompanying noises, subtleties and not-so-subtle cues, I found them to be confusing. It was a bit like translating Greek, a language I do not speak. I was unsure what

> *So sit down, be quiet and ask, "What's here?"*

the different messages meant. For example, at first I spent a lot of time simply asking my body what I was feeling. Apparently I had paid so little attention to my feelings I wasn't even sure which one was which. I discovered an important rule: *If you don't know what you feel, you don't know what you need.*

For me, just the act of stopping and dropping my attention into my body was challenging. I like to stay in motion. I felt that stopping meant I was missing out or not being productive. In any case, when I listened, I heard, *You're tired! A lot.* I didn't like it, but only until I made myself sick from *not* listening did I really get that my body *never* lies.

Next arose the lifetime of unexpressed emotion, hurt, anger, and pain. Oh boy, this was heavy and scary. I had not wanted to feel it when it originally happened, and I was really not excited about feeling the backlog the second time around. But I was on a mission, and so feel I did—for two years. Every time I stopped to listen, I got tears and tears and tears and rage and rage and feelings I thought would never end. Yet the more I felt, the more I emptied out, the more at peace with myself and the world around me I felt! And yes, despite the onslaught of seeming never-ending emotion, it did end. And then when I felt more stable emotionally (when I felt *not crazy*), I began to ask *different* questions, like, *What is my life work and purpose?* After getting more clarity there, I simply began asking, on a daily basis or whenever an emotion came up, *What do I need to know right now?* Currently, this is my most favorite question.

> *If you only experience one moment of peace, that is enough. One genuine moment is a tremendous gift.* 🜋

Everyone is different, and there is no wrong way to do this, so try it out! (See chapter 11 for more resources on the SHOMI® method.)

If you can only do one minute at a time, that's better than not at all, and life will promptly reward you. You may notice changes immediately. If you only experience one moment of peace, that is enough. One genuine moment is a tremendous gift. To take an audible breath, a sigh, to relax your shoulders—these are gifts as well. And that's how the SHOMI® method works. Try it, and remember: what you give yourself you get back.

Grounding

As you become more sophisticated in your practice, you might start learning how to ground yourself—to connect to the planet. While there are many ways to help you ground yourself, I like to simply sit, be quiet, and drop an imaginary gold cord through the floor connecting me to the center of the earth. Then simply breathe and allow the energy to come from the center of the earth and mingle and awaken my life force, creating a kind of relaxed awareness that I call presence! And then, just ask and listen.

As you progress and become more comfortable with sitting with yourself, you will begin to learn your own body's unique language and receive more and more answers. Sitting quietly, undistracted, with yourself is a worthwhile investment. As I've mentioned, the way you treat yourself is the same way others will treat you.

Imagine: if we had learned this tool early on, perhaps we would have listened to our own truths—what our bodies were trying to tell us—instead of making our ways through the obstacle course of our mind's rationalizations and lies.

The SHOMI® Steps

1. Find a quiet place where you won't be distracted, and sit with yourself.
2. Ask, *What's here?* or *What do I need to know right now?*
3. Listen.
4. Notice sensations, feelings, images or words that may come.
5. Follow your body's impeccable wisdom.
6. Do this every day, maybe several times a day.

That's it! You have a powerful practice. Yes, the mind wants to know how to do it *right*, but don't worry about what's *right*. You will catch on and realize that "doing it right" is yet another stalling tactic to avoid sitting down in that scary silence and being with yourself in that nothingness: a way to skirt all that pain that you think will take your last breath; a way to keep at bay the self-loathing you're afraid will consume you, or the rage you're afraid will hurt yourself or someone else. We all have all of that. But, if we don't take the time to feel it, our stuffed emotions will find myriad ways to sabotage our relationships and numb our ability to love and to feel loved.

I have some suggestions for ways to let these feelings out safely.

My First Time Feeling

Depending on what you have been through and how much emotion you have stuffed, the intensity of this process will vary in the beginning. I can tell you that at first, sitting with myself, being present with the huge backlog of feelings I had stuffed down over the years, was terrifying. I had hidden rage at being sexually abused, beaten and neglected. I had all the tears I had never cried because I was too busy trying to survive, because I had become numb, because I was ashamed, because I thought if I cried all those tears I would never stop. I honestly thought if I allowed myself to feel, maybe my tears would kill me or I would go into a depression and never come out. I was afraid that maybe I would hurt someone if I expressed my disappointment and anger, or that no one would like or love me if I expressed my real feelings. I had a million reasons and fears at first, all of which were the lies I told myself—and ultimately what kept me from the freedom I have today, the authentic freedom of being.

Never mind that I had never sat with myself in silence before. Sure, I had meditated, but the goal in that was to quiet my mind, not to listen to my body, not to feel whatever was inside of me. Before, I was trying to change who I was, not sit quietly and be with her. I had come to believe that feelings were a weakness and for wimpy, needy, overly feminine types, not for me. Until, of course, I realized that this stoic, in control, I-can-handle-it attitude was exactly what had cut me off from feeling at all. So I let it blow—all of it!

The first time I practiced this body-centered self inquiry, I trusted my intuition and found someone to bear witness. I thought, in case I freaked out, I had better have someone on call. Depending on the intensity of your past and the level to which you have stuffed your emotions, you too may want to arrange for some initial support. I asked a woman I knew who was nonjudgmental, open-minded and capable of holding this kind of space, a safe place to feel all the way out loud. She was trained in body-centered therapy and had years and years of experience bearing witness to people's different processes of unraveling what was buried inside.

Her office was in the woods, and I went late on a Sunday night. I wasn't sure exactly what I needed, but I knew enough to set a few ground rules so I would feel comfortable and safe. I asked that she under no circumstances take me to a loony bin and have me locked up. This was a real fear of mine, and I made her promise she would not do so. Also, she was not to touch me, and I didn't have to look at her. I only wanted her there so I wouldn't hurt myself, and so in case I would go crazy, I would have someone who could bring me home or would know what to do. She agreed. I could see in her face that I could trust her.

And just so you know I know how unbelievably scary this all is: All I could do at first was shake my fists. My back was turned to her. I was standing up and that's all I could do for the first ten minutes, I was so frozen and shut down. She asked me, in a very gentle voice, one simple question that sent me into orbit, something I had never before considered: "What do your fists want to say?"

And that was it, like someone had given me permission to tell the truth and wanted in earnest to hear the answer—without punishing me or leaving me, or making me wrong, or telling me I was a whack job or too sensitive or had PMS or was angry or insecure or crazy or whatever. What came out of me was absolutely no less than sonic. The sounds scared me almost to death. I screamed and cried so loudly I honestly thought someone would call the police or that I would explode for real into a thousand pieces.

Over the next two hours my body shook, quaked and rolled all over the room as I cried and screamed and laughed—yes, laughed hysterically—and yelled and swore. Then I finally fell to the ground, empty and relieved in a way that I had not ever experienced. After I lay there for a while in the silence that enveloped me, I realized that I did not die, that my feelings didn't suffocate and kill me. I discovered that feelings don't disappear when you numb them; they just wait in the body to be felt. It is then and only then that they can finally be released. While they were painful, I now knew that they were only feelings, not to be feared but to be *felt* all the way. And while I knew there was more in there, I had let the proverbial lid off, and intuitively knew this was a major key to staying awake and present to my authentic self. Lying in the afterglow, all I could think was, "When can I do this again?"

I saw her six more times, same place and time, each time an out-pouring of whatever my body and spirit had to say, scream or feel all the way out loud! Until I felt comfortable enough sitting alone with myself, knowing if, at any time, I needed to, I could call on her to be my witness. Yes, my witness: someone who could see all of me—ugly and hideous and pathetic or whatever my judgments were—and not make them mean anything. Someone who could simply see this as a natural letting-go of what my body had been holding onto for years and what needed to be cleared out! Someone who could be there with me until I could do the same for myself by myself.

The benefits were immediate and obvious, so obvious that family and friends started saying things like, "You seem so happy, so calm, so at peace, in your body, grounded"—things no one had ever said about me before. They had said I was intense and funny, beautiful and driven, but now they were seeing my inner beauty, who I really was. Who I had been afraid I was—flawed and unlovable—turned out not to be the case! And more, the glow, the love that radiated—it lasted longer and longer each time I took care to drop in and clear out my body and feel my feelings. It was better than what I dreamed of; it truly was Happily Ever After, inside of me!

WHAT IS INSIDE OF YOU?

Now it's time for you to consider what is inside of you, and what you may need so that you can be with it, to feel it, maybe for the very first time. Even if you're afraid to face what's waiting for you—history, hurt feelings, anger, resentment of your own—you can get to the other side if you have the courage to go within! Perhaps you need an enlightened witness, a therapist or counselor, a guide, someone well trained in body-centered work, or simply a friend who will simply be with you, without judgment. You can try Gabrielle Roth's Shamanic moving meditation (the 5Rhythms), Osho's Dynamic Meditations, the Hakomi method, or make up your own; the point is—*feel* it all the way out loud! Whatever you choose, it is what there is to do. Go sit down (or stand) and be with it. Feel it. It is the bridge that will take you from where you are to where you want to be. It is *yourself* that you seek. Begin a Daily Practice. This practice will become the container, the belt, that holds all the exercises, tools and skills you will need to create healthy relationships.

Don't just talk about it, SHOMI®! This is a practice of self-inquiry that will remove the obstacles to everything you ever wanted. All you have to do is *begin within*!

Chapter Four

The Mirror

*No positive change can occur in your life
as long as you cling to the thought that the reason
for your not living well lies outside of yourself.*
—IRVIN YALOM

Laurel was six feet tall, gorgeous by almost anyone's standards, and had a heart made of gold. Raised on a farm in the Midwest, she worked hard and played hard, and she had her sights set on living the American dream. Popular in every way, she was definitely someone most likely to succeed. Life was hers for the taking, but somehow it took her instead.

Many years after my own wake-up call, one spring morning, as things were just starting to bloom and come alive, the phone rang. It was my best girlfriend on the other end, calling to see if I had a hit on where our friend Laurel might be. She had apparently taken off, leaving her twin three-year-old girls home alone, and had been missing now for two days. My friend knew I could be pretty intuitive, and called to see if anything came up for me as she recounted a few details about the night Laurel vanished.

I knew she had been having problems with her husband, so my first thought was that they had gotten into a fight. I headed upstairs with the phone in my hand, my mind buzzing, not quite as concerned as my friend seemed to be, thinking our pal probably took off for a few days to teach her husband a lesson. As far as most of us girls were concerned, he had not been the most noble or agreeable of partners, so it didn't seem unlikely she would have needed some space, even though it seemed totally out of character for her to leave her twin girls home alone.

Theirs was a relationship not dissimilar to that of many others who had built theirs based largely on chemistry, excitement and control. Passionate, dramatic, rocky to say the least, but apparently it had gotten pretty bad lately.

> *Loving yourself is the essential foundation for ALL relationships.*
> 𝓜

I was in my closet now. "You know, I just see a guy with dark hair, maybe a goatee, I don't know," I said hanging up some clothes that were in a heap on the settee in my closet. But I did know, I saw something else, something more than a man's face, something so dark that I had to erase it; and yet, as soon as I tried to reach for it again—poof, it was gone.

"Come on, I can hear it in your voice," my friend said.

"I dunno, I mean . . . yeah, okay, I saw drugs or something. That's pretty much it, but she wasn't into drugs unless I am missing something. Did she start doing drugs lately?" I asked trying to further erase that icky, dark feeling my initial hit gave me.

"No, she has been drinking a lot lately, but…I don't know, it's just not like her. We were talking about going away together only two days ago and . . . it's so weird!" she said, worried.

"Look, call me tomorrow and let me know what you hear. I will sit with this, and if anything else comes, I will call you, okay? Let's try not to worry! I am sure she just took off to teach him a lesson, you know, to shake him up," I said half-heartedly; in the other half of my heart I dared not look.

"Yeah, but the twins—she would never just leave the twins like that," she said.

"I know. Look, don't think about it; its too negative to go there. Just say some prayers. It's going to be fine, okay?"

"Yeah, I know. Okay, talk later then." We hung up. I noticed my cats going crazy, orbiting around like they could see something I couldn't. I thought it was strange, but I didn't read too much into it. I told myself Laurel would show up.

Two days later the phone rang. "Maryanne . . ."

"Hi," I said anticipating the worst from her tone, "What's happening?"

"They found her . . . they found her bo . . . her body." My friend could hardly get the words out.

My eyes immediately filled with tears but I raised my hand and shouted, "NO!" as though I could

> *A practice of self-care is a CRITICAL act of responsibility, not selfishness.* 🜔

stop the truth of what she was saying. "No, you're not telling me this! Stop it!" She began to moan, and I reminded myself she was my best friend's best friend since high school. I caught my flow of feeling, patted my chest, cleared my throat and pulled myself together. "Talk to me, tell me what's happening, what do we know?"

I could hear her trying to catch her breath. "They found her body in a field about a . . . mile . . . from—" she broke down crying again. "About a mile from the house . . . She . . . had her ID and . . . flipflops on . . . I don't understand why she would have her ID and flipflops on. This can't be happening!" she wailed.

I paused, not sure what was happening myself. "Do they know anything? I mean, do they have any idea of why she was there, honey?" I asked as tenderly as possible.

"Uhhmm . . ." She tried to gather her thoughts. "They are saying they think it's a suicide . . . that she committed suicide . . . Oh my God . . . she would never do that . . . Laurel would never kill herself. He did this! . . . I know . . . he did this, Maryanne . . . She would never leave those kids alone and go off to some field. She spent ten years trying to get pregnant with that asshole, and she would never just leave them there!" she screamed.

"What do you mean 'just leave them,' honey?" I asked again.

"They are saying that she called Roger—no, that *he said* she called him and said that she was going to hurt herself or something, because she sent a friend an email saying she couldn't take it anymore, and then she called him and asked him to come get the kids. 'Cause she moved out, you know, and he's mad and doesn't want her to divorce him. I don't know . . . I can't believe this is all happening!"

> *You can't give what you don't have.*
>
> ₥

I was feverishly trying to put the pieces together. "Who's 'they,' honey, who did Roger tell this to… the police?"

"Yeah, the police."

"Okay, so they found her. And did they do an autopsy already? I mean," I slowed down. "Do they know what happened?" I asked carefully. I had no idea how to ask such delicate questions. It was, if nothing else, incredibly awkward.

"No. I mean, no, I don't know. I guess they will tell us more later. I just found this out now," she said.

I could hear her start to collapse. "Okay, honey, so what do we need to do? Where's her mom? How is she? I mean, who is with her?"

"The girls are with her—Jen and Mel and her Dad—and I'm going up there now!" she trailed off.

"Do you want me to come?" I was ready to drop whatever.

"No, it's okay, I'm on my way now. I will call you when I know more, okay?"

"Okay, be careful driving. Call me when you get up there. I am right here, baby girl, okay?" I said, desperate to find any way to comfort her.

"'kay, call you in . . . later." She fumbled with the phone, and the line went dead. I hung up the phone, stunned. There were no words to describe the dread that filled my body, the anguish I could feel that engulfed my soul sister and best friend. I just kept shaking my head. I couldn't believe it; I'm not sure I can, even now.

The next week was overflowing with gruesome and baffling details. All of us who knew and cared for Laurel tried to make sense of it, yet it made no sense at all. My girlfriend who saves everything had amassed a pile of pictures chronicling Laurel's life from childhood through her fortieth year. One morning, in the midst of her grief, she brought me a picture of Laurel and me from the last time the three of us were all together. She handed it to me like it

> *People treat you the way you treat yourself.*

was a newborn baby. I took it in the same manner, staring at it blankly. Somehow, seeing her, seeing us together, brought up the unbearable feelings of horror and grief I had initially tried to stuff. There she was, staring right at me, her arms around my waist, smiling her million-dollar smile as though it were only yesterday. And now—just like that—she was gone.

My girlfriend and I stood together in my office doorway, sobbing belly-to-belly as we held on to each other for dear life. The thought that anyone so close could simply disappear like that, that life really is this fragile, that all we have is right now, was almost unbearable. I will never forget that tender moment. Within it lay a heartbeat that we all share, a place permanently connected, pulsing relentlessly while the rest of time just stood there and watched.

We melted out of our embrace and silently sorted through some of the other snapshots, enduring glimpses of our sister's half-lived life. The obvious did not escape us, that she was a raving beauty queen—a blue-eyed goddess. But her gentle nature and unique radiance was even more beautiful than that. Somehow her gentleness made the loss of her seem more horrifying. Though she was almost embarrassed by her beauty, you would have never known it, given her self-confident nature. An enigma, as most women are, she was a cheerleader who drove a Ducati and laughed at it all. But if you looked closely, as the years passed, you could see the light dim in her eyes; that sparkly little girl filled with dreams and mischief fell farther and farther away. Her smile became reflexive, her postures uninspired, her radiance diminished with each passing year— an easily overlooked cry for help.

We talked and talked, guessed and conjectured for hours in the days that followed, hoping to find some shred, some clue as to what really happened to Laurel. Not one of us wanted to believe a relationship gone bad would ever lead to this. As the story unraveled, one person at a time, it turns out that no beauty, no chemistry, no success, no perfect picture was great enough, strong enough, real enough to comfort her unrequited love. She had done everything right, she thought: she loved him; was a good wife, mother and hostess; kept their finances; attended to his needs. Her silent scream was now permanently silenced; the angels had accompanied her home, where she would have everlasting peace, we all hoped.

> *Being externally*
> *referenced is*
> *OLD SCHOOL!* ♡ℳ

HINDSIGHT: LOVE YOUR SELF

Like so many of us, Laurel had spent many precious years trying to figure out how to love and be loved; seeking to find a relationship with someone handsome, tall and strong, someone to start a life with, a family with, to build their dreams together and with whom to live Happily Ever After. She didn't know about loving herself; she was raised to be loved by others. She didn't have the tools in this book. She didn't have a daily self-care practice. Laurel assumed most men were capable of being loyal and trustworthy, and by nature, capable of integrity. She was taught that most men settled down when they fall in love and get married; that it's important to be a tiger in the bedroom and a saint in the kitchen; it's as easy to marry a rich man as a poor one, that men don't want women with a past, that it's a man's world, and so on. Consequently, we learned to muffle our needs and to please men (and everyone else) instead.

I don't know for certain, but there is solid evidence that Laurel compromised herself over and over again in the name of love and her commitment to her family. Despite her mother's best intentions, Laurel didn't have relationship role models that encouraged her to leave a bad relationship. Like most of us, her mother and her mother's mother were likely encouraged by example to work it out, to change somehow to become more worthy of a man's

> *Great relationships begin within!* ❀

love. She was told that the way to get him to stop behaving badly or to be different was to give more—more sex, more devotion, more children, more attention—by changing herself to meet his needs. She lost respect for herself little by little until she, like millions of women, suffered from anxiety and depression. I believe this is largely due to lack of self-care and a vigilant, Daily Practice of self-love! In Laurel's world, she would likely have been considered selfish, self-centered—or worse, a bitch— had she put her needs in proper perspective. (In my experience a large percentage of women would rather be called a whore than a bitch.)

Suffice it to say, the damage was done: most of us were already pro-grammed to please even as the women's liberation movement flowered. The divorce rate escalated as women fled for their lives. *You've come a long way, baby*, the ads said; we could vote, smoke, drink, divorce and even have sex without getting pregnant or being married. So they said. *Free at last*. But were we?

Our cultural conditioning remains stronger than ever. The diet and makeup industries alone show us the billions and billions of dollars we invest every year keeping alive our programming to be externally referenced—meaning we refer to the world outside ourselves for our value, rather than using our own wisdom and guidance for recognition. This external referencing is a genetic cocktail energized by one part endurance, the other part survival.

It is my sincere hope that instead of staying asleep to our needs, we take the opportunity we have today, right now, six feet *above* ground, to count our blessings and begin or continue the journey inward. Do it for Laurel, for all the Laurels, and most of all, for yourself and the generations to come. If Laurel had the tools I am about to share with you, she might be here with us today.

THE FIRST TOOL: THE MIRROR

The first tool for your Relationship Tool Belt is the Mirror, which represents *loving yourself.* Upon my own awakening, I recognized two things right away. First, that how I felt about myself was mirrored proportionately in all my relationships. Soon after that, I made the real connection that changing the way I treated myself was the key to a loving, lasting relationship. Needless to say, I did not treat myself in loving ways, quite the contrary! I was mean to myself, had little tolerance for my sensitivities or weaknesses, was very insecure, had low self-worth and a ridiculously long list of expectations, starting with being perfect.

So many of us, including Laurel, have been programmed to be externally referenced. We try to find something outside ourselves for our source of love, happiness and fulfillment. We have all bought into the same Happily-Ever-After programming, instead of recognizing the greater truth—that loving ourselves is a verb and a noun. When we love ourselves enough to sit with ourselves, to look inside ourselves, we will find what we are actually looking for: *true* love.

You need to take responsibility for giving yourself what you want most. Changing this one fundamental way of thinking and being is critical to your success in almost every area of life. The good news is that it is achievable. The bad news, for a lot of us, is that it can be hard. We are so used to the way things are, and we are addicted to believing that if we change something outside of us—*him*, our circumstances, our appearance—we will be okay. Then, and only then—if we are lucky—will we live Happily Ever After.

I am saying that what we want is within reach, in each and every one of us, and that maybe we just don't know it. More likely, we just go about getting it in all the wrong ways. That's why I am reaching out to you—so, like me, you will have the chance to change your reality, to rewrite the script! I am saying that

> *I made the real connection that changing the way I treated myself was the key to a loving, lasting relationship.*

Great Relationships Begin Within, and that when we know, as *foresight*, that the source of true love is inside of us, we will begin to create the rest of our experience from a more solid base of self-esteem and self-respect. And while it is important to love and care for others, it is fundamental to love ourselves first, as we cannot give what we don't have.

Turning this tool into a skill has taken me years, but I can say every ounce of effort has paid off tenfold! Understanding that *I* was the source of true love, that I was the problem *AND* the solution, was liberating.

The sooner you can embrace this gigantic truth, that what you seek is inside yourself, the quicker you will be able to attract and create what you really want. You will begin to stop looking outside yourself to be fulfilled, so you can take time and choose a partner who is a good match, has a healthy Relationship Tool Belt himself, and the skills to help the relationship work over the long haul, rather than choosing a childhood fairy tale or unrealistic need. The law of attraction makes this point beautifully: "Energy flows where attention goes." We will attract that which we focus on, so we must be careful to attend to what is really important. As they say, "If we don't do the work, we will get more of what we've got!"

So take a good look in your metaphorical Mirror and if you don't like what you see, change your relationship with yourself and the world around you will change, too! Whatever you want to attract in your life—all you have to do is *be* that! More about this concept in the chapters to come, but for now I just want you to start looking—and seeing.

EXERCISE: TAKE STOCK

Those who cannot remember the past are condemned to repeat it.
—GEORGE SANTAYANA

One day I called a friend who was a brilliant doctor, yet, like so many women, emotionally handicapped when it came to relationships.

"Candace," I said, breathless, as though I had just discovered the cure for male infidelity. "Do you have a piece of paper and a pen?" I hadn't even said hello.

"Yeah, got it, go!" she said. I loved that about her. No matter how busy she was she didn't even question my motive.

"Okay, draw a house," I ordered anxiously.

"A house?"

"No wait, okay." That was too complicated. "Okay, draw a pyramid," I said, drawing one myself so I could walk her through it.

"Done."

"Okay, now draw four or five horizontal or perpendicular—no, horizontal lines across the pyramid, making, you know . . . sections. Do you get it?"

"Uh-huh," she said, obviously doing it.

"Okay, now, at the bottom of the pyramid, write—in one sentence or a word or phrase—what you focus most of your attention on." I waited.

"What do you mean?"

"I mean, from the time you wake up in the morning, what do you spend your time thinking about or focusing on: like, how you look, your weight, work, your son, what? Tell the truth, because this is critical."

"Hang on," she said, and muffled her phone for twenty seconds. "Okay, I'm back."

"What did you put? No, don't tell me, it doesn't matter...Just do the same thing all the way up to the top of the pyramid and tell me when you're done."

"I'll call you back," she said perfunctorily, and hung up. I couldn't wait. I paced around my office for the next fifteen minutes, making occasional notes. The phone rang.

"It's me . . . so now what?"

"So this, plain and simple, is a representation of what we value most; and it shows us where we spend our energy."

"All right," she said, unsure if this was my point.

"But the thing is . . . do you know the story of the Big Bad Wolf?" I asked.

"Yeah, sure."

"Well, let's say this pyramid is your house and the Big Bad Wolf comes by. And he can blow your house down, take you out of the game, by—wait a minute, what was at the base of your pyramid?"

"Uhh . . . my body and physical appearance, I guess."

"Right, that's what I had too, isn't that crazy?" I was thinking that was probably most women's greatest energy expense and they didn't even know it. "Anyway, let's say the big bad wolf is your boyfriend, and all he has to do is say, "You're fat!" to devastate you and blow your house down. Then he cheats on you or leaves you because you're not turning him on anymore, because your body isn't perfect. Follow me?"

"Yeah, kinda."

"Go back to your paper. Say you have $100 worth of attention to spend a day. Write down how much attention you'll spend on each category every day—like appearance $60, work $45, family $40, and friends

$25. That would add up to $170, which means you'd be $70 overdrawn. The thing is—can we still do this? Are you good?" I asked, aware of the time.

"Yeah, I am on a break. Go."

"When I did this I found out I was totally overdrawn, aside from spending my attention on things that I wasn't particularly proud of. The point is, spending my attention, my precious attention, on my appearance made me vulnerable and insecure all the time. You know, almost anyone could hurt me or make me feel bad."

"Yeah," she replied. "Every time Gary even looks at another woman, I think he likes her because she has a better body and I get jealous. Then I think I should lose some weight or work out more."

> *Taking stock*
> *is a great investment*
> *of your energy.*

"Exactly! I don't want to feel that vulnerable all the time, or let people or circumstances have that much power over me. That's how I came up with this pyramid. Toward the top of my pyramid was 'God, Spirituality' and then it dawned on me—what if I flipped them and put God, The Divine, at the base, made *that* my foundation? Then no one could hurt me. I mean, yes, I would maybe still feel hurt, but God would be the foundation; my inner world would be the foundation instead of my outer world. My foundation would be the unshakable, or at least the most solid, foundation that I can think of. Then no one and no thing could have the power to really hurt me again, not even the big, bad wolf."

"Okay, great. So, how am I going to do that?" she asked.

"Good question. I'll get back to you." I was still working out the details.

Shortly after I hung up I heard the words, *I am moving from being externally referenced to internally referenced!* My life was forever changed. I realized that "taking stock," as I like to call it—seeing where I spend my attention—helps reveal how I spend my energy, giving me a great indication of what my happiness depends on. When I spend as much time as possible on healthy, self-loving things, like God and our creative endeavors and family and friends (in that order), versus when I make others' attention and approval the prime focus of my happiness, I am more likely to thrive and be less vulnerable to being affected so easily by everyone and everything around me!

Taking Stock

Taking stock is such an important element of self-care and self-love. It shows us precisely where we are focusing our effort and energy, which is especially important because energy flows where attention goes. In other words, what you spend your energy on creates more of that. For example, if you spend your time focusing

> *Energy flows where attention goes.*
> 𝓂

on negative things, such as *I'm fat* or *I'm unlovable* or *My life sucks* or *Life is hard*, you will likely attract more of the very thing you are focusing on. If you focus on getting your value from your looks, so will others. If you focus on getting your value from being sexy, so will others. If you focus on being accommodating, everyone will expect you to be.

The next exercise is to simply take a look at what you are focusing on, which will probably explain what is currently being reflected to you in your life. Particularly if you notice that your life is not a reflection of the way you would like it to be! This exercise will quickly and clearly show you where and how you are spending your precious energy and time. You might be surprised; you might even be amazed!

Before you begin, know that it is imperative for you to be honest with yourself. No one will ever see this; you can even burn the evidence! It is for you and you alone, but you will cheat yourself if you are not completely honest.

The Big Bad Wolf Exercise

1. Get a sheet of paper, 8.5 by 11 is fine. (In fact, there will be a need for paper throughout this book, so you may want to get an entire pad to have handy. I don't recommend a journal, because you will want to have loose pages.)

2. Draw a large triangle, taking up the whole page (see diagram below).

3. Next, draw several horizontal lines (about four to six).

4. On the bottom (largest) line, write one word or a phrase that describes where you spend most of your energy and time; for example, Physical Appearance. (This is a common one—looking in the mirror, thinking about your body, your weight, exercising, thinking about people looking at you, shopping for clothes, getting beauty treatments, working so you can buy more of the above, hoping men will notice you, getting attention, etc.) As I said, be honest!

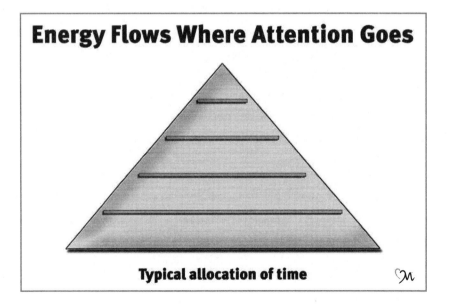

Energy Flows Where Attention Goes

Typical allocation of time

Another example: Finding a Relationship (spending time on the prowl, getting ready so you can attract someone, reading about it, daydreaming about it, fantasizing, exercising, dieting, coloring your hair, ritually putting on makeup, flirting, going to places hoping men will be there, etc.—whatever is true for you). Where do you believe your primary expenditure of energy really is? Not where you would *like* it to be, where it *is*.

Notice that dieting and exercising could fall under Physical Appearance, Finding a Relationship, or Health. Sometimes it is not immediately obvious which one it should go under until you look at what is *underneath* all your behaviors. That's where you will find the true intention and motivating force behind your actions.

5. Next, go to the space above that in your triangle and do the same thing. Write a phrase or word describing where you are next likely to spend your energy, and so on up the ladder, in order from the most time to the least time spent.

    Here's an example of a completed triangle, from least to most energy spent:

    *   Spiritual pursuit (least amount of time focused on)
    *   Career
    *   Social life
    *   Appearance (most time focused on)

Here's another example:

- Self-improvement
- Career
- Social life
- Exercise
- Relationship

And another:

- God
- Aging
- Loveless relationship
- Financial insecurity
- Other people's needs

Your triangle will be unique to you!

6. As you review what you've written in your triangle—which, as I said may be a surprise—let's imagine that each item has been assigned a percentage of energy expenditure. For instance, Physical Appearance, 45 percent; Career, 30 percent; Social Life, 25 percent; Self-Development, 10 percent; which adds up to—oops—110 percent. In this case, if your energy was money in a checking account, you would be overdrawn!

SELF-INQUIRY

What do you notice about how you spend your time and how much time you spend? How does it make you *feel* when you look at your triangle? How sturdy is your foundation? Is there some connection you can make with what your parents valued and where you focus your attention? Do you notice any resistance to looking at yourself honestly and without reserve?

As I explained to Candace, if the foundation of your house was your appearance, and on top of that your career, and so forth, and the Big Bad Wolf came along, he would be able to blow your house down or take you out of the game, simply by telling you that you are not attractive enough. Any blow that takes your foundation right out from beneath you could knock your "house" down. In other words, if your foundation is made up of insecurity and vanity, it is not impervious. It is vulnerable to criticism and rejection, to bringing the whole house down.

Worse yet, if you get involved with a wolf who values the same superficial and unstable things you do, then what? And isn't that exactly what we do? Instead of changing our values, we chase the wolf relentlessly, trying to get him to love and approve of us—the pigs that we think we are—in the hope of some day becoming whatever would stop the wolf from constantly blowing our house apart. (Since the house is a metaphor for *you,* blowing your house apart means blowing *you* apart.) And then we watch him wreak havoc all over town with our sister, mother, friends and every other woman we know, all believing that if we just lost or gained more weight, were a little more accommodating, or more subservient or selfless, that he would finally love us.

For me this recurrent scenario would no longer do. I did not like what I saw or felt when I did this exercise, and I was prepared to do what it took to change my life entirely. My foundation inside of me—my values and where I spent my energy—was weak and it created a veritable house of cards. I spent most of my attention trying to fix my appearance, believing that if I were thinner or prettier I would then be lovable. Next, I focused on my career, thinking that if, and when, I became someone, then I would be worthy and lovable. I worked my way up the ladder until my pyramid looked like this:

- God
- Friends
- Career
- Relationship
- Self-image

The question is, are you willing to look and do what it takes to change your pyramid?

After seeing this myself, I promptly began the process of changing my thinking! I started a two-year process devoted to spending large amounts of time learning about myself, loving myself and connecting with God. I realized this investment was the best use of my time and the foundation on which I could ultimately rest my entire life and self. No one could truly harm me again in the same ways I had allowed!

Today my pyramid looks like this:
- Play/friends
- Career
- Health
- Family/relationship
- Spirituality/growth and personal development

I took myself for long walks, spoke to myself lovingly, and covered my mirrors with powerful, loving quotes written on construction paper. I began to focus all that attention on myself in constructive, loving ways. Things began to change dramatically, mostly because I was on a mission and believed it would take no less than this level of effort to create what I really wanted—true love, starting with me! The first time I felt this way was a bit of miracle, but I knew that to sustain it or recreate it was going to take some work.

I didn't want to spend entire days feeling inadequate or fat or unworthy, or sitting by the phone waiting for someone to call me to tell me they loved me so I could feel okay. I wanted to feel okay all by myself, and I was fiercely determined to have that. And so I did! I began living as though energy does flow where attention goes. I know now that this is not a cliché; it's one of the highest truths. When I switched my attention and focus from what was fragile, fleeting and unstable to what I knew to be lasting, solid, stable and truly beautiful, all my energy moved in the direction of my attention. Then, amazingly, I saw the energy of the people around me begin to switch to a deeper recognition of what was truly important to me, without me saying a thing. The result was that I had me now! I finally wanted to be me, not someone else.

> *The strongest, most unshakable foundation is inside of you!*
> ℳ

I invite you to evaluate what your personal foundation is made up of, whether you, too, are vulnerable to the Big Bad Wolf. If so, take this opportunity to shift where your attention goes and, consequently, where your energy flows, so that you can become unshakable!

BUILDING A STRONG FOUNDATION

As my girlfriend Candace put it, "So now what do I do? How *do* I change this pyramid around?" Self-inquiry, the better to see you with, my dear. Oh, sorry, wrong fairy tale. This is no fairy tale; this is the hardcore, direct route to the highest truth of who you are—your authentic self—where lies your intuition and your greatest of all strengths. *How do I change the pyramid?* The Daily Practice of self-inquiry! This was the vehicle that escorted me from the externally focused little piggy I was, to the curious, self-inquiring, seeking spirit that I am today.

Having realized that a fast-food mentality had never served me well, I had to look elsewhere. To paraphrase Einstein, doing the same thing over and over was only going to bring me the same results. So I looked inside, deep, deep inside—where few of us want or dare to go—because we are afraid we will find that we are flawed and unlovable after all. Maybe that's what you have come to believe. But as much as I have ever been sure of anything, I know this to be true: until you believe you are perfect and lovable the way you are, no one else will believe it either. If you want or need to build a stronger foundation, begin the journey deep and deeper inside. The only way out of pain, as they say, is through it. So jump in, feet first. When I did, much to my surprise I came through the other side wiser for it. You will too.

Don't just talk about it…SHOMI®.

Chapter Five

The Magnet

The thing that brings you together in unconsciousness
will be the thing that pulls you apart.
—RELATIONSHIP RESEARCH INSTITUTE

A devoted mother of three and a Ph.D., Mia served on the boards of high-profile nonprofits. She was a loyal wife and vigilant caretaker of their blind daughter, and a true friend, as down-to-earth a woman as they come. She had spent her entire adult life being a woman of integrity and commitment and was on a sure path of personal development. She was no stranger to the concept of self-love and had an inordinate supply of self-esteem. And while she had her own set of issues, some of them whoppers, Mia was about to make one of the biggest leaps in her life—the leap from being committed to taking care of *them* first, to being committed to *herself* first.

Mia had a great, big tool belt when it came to personal development in just about every area, except when it came to her husband Brandt. I hesitated to pick up my cell phone when it rang one day. I knew who it was and what it was about; and frankly, I was tired of "the story." I wondered when she would be, too. But I answered the phone despite myself.

"What's up?" I said, as I do when I want someone to get to the point sooner rather than later.

I could hear Mia sniffle. "He's gone . . . he's moving out . . . he's coming back for the rest of his things next week."

Pause. A slightly different twist on the story this time. I had confronted the man only a few days before, to suggest that he admit to Mia that he was having an affair—and to do it quickly, because I didn't like seeing my friend suffer. I also mentioned to this person, who was "finding himself" (which apparently involved bonking his secretary; perhaps he thought he would find himself inside *her* vagina), that the definition of evil is *intentionally invalidating another person's intuition.*

"Okay," I said. I couldn't help thinking of the favor he was doing her by leaving, no matter how frightened or bad she felt now.

Her voice quivered. "Twenty-six years down the toilet. I don't know who I am without him."

I felt she was on the right track with the toilet idea. Twenty-six years spent giving, giving, giving to this lying, cheating, energy-sucking child of a man. I could hardly wait for her to see what I saw: a vivacious, talented, loving woman worthy of having a loving partnership, rather than the broken-down, used up, middle-aged woman she had let him convince her she was.

"Did you close the bank accounts?"

"Did I what?" she asked, confused by my blunt question.

"Mia . . . did . . . you . . . close . . . the bank accounts?"

"No . . . why?"

"Mia, hello? What does Brandt's behavior tell you about Brandt? Come on, Mia! That he's a narcissist, which means that he only thinks about himself, which means—"

"Okay, okay, but why would he close the bank accounts?"

"Listen to me: This is the man who, for the third time (that I knew of) lied about his emotional involvement with another woman. The same man who swore on his life that he wasn't having sex with her, so technically that meant he wasn't cheating on you . . . again. The same man who told you he wasn't in love with you anymore *five minutes after he made love to you on the beach* just last week—after he came back from a first-class trip spending YOUR money on her! Are you following me here?"

"Yeah . . . but what does that have to do with the bank accounts?" she asked again.

"Oh my gawd, Mia! Wake up, lady! He doesn't care about you right now, and as far as I can tell, has no respect for you. What he *does* have is a new relationship with someone who has expensive tastes and two little kids. Where do you think his first stop is going to be?"

Mia, like my other friends, knew that calling to ask me for relationship advice was lethal, because I would pull no punches. That's the way it was in our friendship. *Note to self: take Maryanne off my list of friends to call when I want to be comforted by bullshit or to have proverbial smoke blown up ass.* That was not my strength. On the other hand, I am the one to call when you actually want to solve a problem, rather than having me listen to you tell the same story of suffering over and over again. I think of myself as more of a results girl; I talk, and you *actively* listen to what I tell you so you can stop suffering.

"Mia, trust me, hang up the phone and go to the bank …NOW! Call me when you have taken your half of the money; then call a kick-ass attorney. If you don't, he will."

You snooze you lose is not exactly what came to mind when she called back two days later.

"Tell me you went to the bank . . . I hope, Mia?" I didn't even say hello.

"Yeah . . . well, I went there today and . . . "

I cut her off. "Today? You just went today? Didn't I tell you . . . arrgh . . . Mia, what did I say? Did I not tell you to go directly to the bank and take care of that?"

She sighed. "I know, I know," she said, the way she did when she felt defeated. She told me that he had (1) taken *all* the money out of their accounts and (2) announced—the same day I warned her to go to the bank—that she should start looking for a job because he was about to quit his.

"I called an attorney and, well, he said that maybe I should wait before I went to the bank and so…" she tried to explain.

"What attorney did you call? What idiot did you speak to, that for a thousand bucks an hour, would advise you to…? Oh never mind, Mia—finish!" I said, too frustrated to speak further.

"Well anyway, I did find out that he is actually seeing her. He admitted it … I mean, I just asked him point blank and he said yes and that he is in love with her. Oh yeah, and that he is going to make a public statement at work and resign from the board," she said without emotion.

"He told you this, or someone said he's going to do this?" I asked, not believing this insipid, cheating, wimp of a liar had the courage to tell her the truth … finally.

"Oh, *he* told me this … today … and that he will be out of town—with her—for the next two weeks."

"Excuse me?"

"So I went to the bank thinking about what you said, and like you said, he had taken everything out of the accounts two days ago."

"Of course he did!" I said, wishing I wasn't so harsh sometimes.

"You know, Mia, for whatever reason, I find I am unable to withhold my feelings about who Brandt is being right now. I am unable to be objective about the situation. He is *being* a complete *asshole!* You should, without further delay, get the toughest son of a bitch, winningest divorce attorney you can find. Did I say NOW? Because you don't get to do this twice. Are you listening? You do not get to get divorced from this twenty-six-year marriage twice. What you do now matters so much that I am telling you to bookmark your feelings about Brandt. We can process the #&$@! out of this later—but dwelling on Brandt and how he really doesn't love this woman or know himself or know what *he* is doing, etc. etc.…well, #&$@! Brandt! Get on with making sure you take care of yourself, because clearly, my friend, he will not be taking care of you.

Does this make sense? Are you registering any of this?"

"Yes . . . yeah. I got it. I will. I know . . . it's just that, well, I think this is a phase he's going through, and—"

"No, Mia, This is *not* a phase, unless twenty-six years of being a self-centered prick can be considered a phase. Now, hang up the phone and dial the number. Call whoever you know that knows someone who knows someone who can help you take care of this mess *now*. And, by the way, telling yourself that Brandt has your best interest at heart is just, unfortunately, a lie you are telling yourself, a lie that you cannot afford to keep rationalizing right now. Just . . . please . . . do what I am telling you. I know it's hard and he intimidates you and all that; but trust me, go get a superstar attorney. Honey, do you trust me?"

"Yes," she answered immediately.

"Mia . . . I have never lied to you. I know you wish I would some-times. Right now, I am telling you something that a year from now will maybe make more sense, but for now you are just going to have to trust me on this!"

"Okay, I'll call," she said, sounding completely deflated.

"Good. This is *your* life, Mia . . . act like it! Okay? Love you, call me later when you know more," I said, wishing I could reach through the phone and pick her up by her bootstraps.

"How can someone be married to someone for twenty-six years and not know them?" Mia asked the next time she called.

"Is that a real question?"

"I have been making excuses for him and me for a quarter of a cen-tury, telling myself that's just the way he is."

"You mean selfish and narcissistic?"

"And I really didn't get it," she continued, not listening to me.

"What do you think happened, Mia?"

"It wasn't always like this. When Brandt and I first had Laura, things were okay—more than okay—they were good." She paused for quite a while, and we just sat together on the phone. "I can remember calling

Brandt and asking him if it was okay if I got a sitter and went to my dance class . . . Oh, yeah, I used to love to dance . . ." she said, fading off as she thought of how much she missed it. "And so I called the agency, and they sent someone out. I remember I felt so guilty, like going to class was selfish. I guess I thought it made me a bad mom. I'll never forget when I got home and . . . and . . ." She started to whimper.

"Oh, God, it was awful . . . I can remember like it was yesterday, looking at Laura and knowing something was wrong when I took her from her crib. It was terrible! Brandt met me at the hospital, and all I kept thinking was how it was my fault. Brandt didn't try and stop me from thinking it, either."

I could sense myriad emotions course through her as her tone rose and fell while she recalled every detail of how the babysitter had shaken her daughter blind that day. "And all these years later, we've never really talked about it . . . that specific part where I felt responsible and . . . he . . . let me. I haven't thought too much about this, either, but I had a funny feeling when I left the baby with the nanny. I couldn't tell if I was just feeling guilty for leaving her for two hours, or . . . there was nothing noticeably weird about the sitter. I kept telling myself that she was from a reputable agency. I don't know. I guess I never actually looked back in a way—it was too painful, and I've spent the last twenty-whatever years trying to make up for it, with everybody."

"Makes sense," I said.

"What?"

"That you blamed yourself for Laura being blind and have spent most of your adult life believing that taking care of yourself (instead of someone else) is not only *not* okay, but fatal. Not to mention your predisposition to codependence, thus sealing the deal that your life would never—could never—be about you. But mostly because you believed it was true that you were to blame," I said gently.

"What do you mean?"

"We buy into other people's projections from an early age. We learn that what love looks like is to make your mom and dad happy, or else they will not love you or they will take their love away. Depending on how healthy your folks were, most of them played some version of this game: 'Be a good girl, you get love; not good, no love.' So in your case, you start trying to please your mom—an alcoholic—as though it's possible to please one! Moms teach us how to love and care for ourselves, so you learned that caring for yourself meant pleasing and caring for your mom. So, on we go with this pattern ingrained, unless we are lucky to find some enlightened witness early on who really sees us and reflects our beauty, and respects us and shows us what unconditional love is. Well, you missed out on that, right?"

"Yeah, right."

"Incidentally, the father is ideally the one who initiates you into relationships with others, follow me?"

"Yep."

"Okay so here's the giant leap: Had you not had your programming and had Brandt not had his, you both may have been two very loving people living a very usual life, going to work and dance classes on occasion. And you still might have encountered the woman who shook your baby. I'm not saying that such a trauma wouldn't have affected you if you had been in a loving relationship—how could it not? But because you were predisposed to feeling that it was in your best interest to take care of everyone else first, it blinded you to the truth. You came away from this horrible thing that happened to your child with a reinforced belief that you shouldn't do things for yourself. But the real truth is that you can't give what you don't have, and being committed to yourself, to the truth of who you are, is part of the foundation for having a healthy relationship. Most of us didn't learn that as girls, and as much as Brandt is on my #&$@! list, this is really about you being committed to you, taking care of you. Because until you do, Mia, no one else will either—not really, my love! To thine own self be true."

She sighed and paused for a moment letting the insight settle. "Thank you, Maryanne, for always, always telling me the truth! I love you for that."

Mia had taken my "Great Relationships Begin Within: Find the Man, Get the Man, Keep the Man" seminar during this whole ordeal, hoping secretly to find out how to keep the man. Instead, she fell in love with herself.

HINDSIGHT:
THERE IS NO "WE" WITHOUT "ME"

Mia's story is a heart-wrenching example of how women feel torn between their commitment to others and their commitment to themselves. Like most of us, Mia did not intend for her life to become a cliché, filled with tragedy, infidelity and loss. She, too, started out with good intentions; and she was already committed to a path of growth and self-inquiry. She did love herself and her husband; however, love by her old definition was not enough to help her sustain and grow a healthy, fulfilling relationship. In the intense day-to-day balancing act required by most of us women who are trying to take care of ourselves, our partner's needs, our children, and work—as well as all the other demands we face in a relationship—our commitment to ourselves is NOT encouraged. Yet it is crucial to our being in integrity with ourselves. As I always say, there is no "we" without "me."

Trying to navigate or attract a healthy, loving, fulfilling relationship without being committed to yourself is like taking a supporting role in your own movie where you should be the leading lady. Mia is a well-educated, passionate woman who has good self-esteem and a practice of self-care; yet after she marries, it becomes harder and harder to be a priority in her own life. She watches her commitments to herself start to wane at every turn and succumbs to letting her husband and family's needs envelop her own. Eventually she disappears in the face of a very traumatic event, validating her false belief that when she chooses herself first, bad things happen.

Do bad things happen to people who are committed to, and take care of, themselves? Yes. But bad things also happen to people who don't take care of themselves, perhaps in greater measure. And this is a story about learning to tell the difference between our intuition and our inner critic—knowing what we are committed to and *why*, and operating from real inner integrity and intention rather than codependence or dependence.

> *A practice of self-care is a CRITICAL act of responsibility, not selfishness.* ꩜

During the course of my seminar, "Great Relationships Begin Within," Mia carefully reviewed her marriage and the day that she made the decision to go to her dance class. While she can't be sure that she would have done anything different in hindsight, she *did* see how difficult it had been for her to feel her intuition, to recognize her feelings as a premonition specific to *this* circumstance, to hear her inner wisdom through the loud haranguing of her inner critic, guilt and rationalizations—which is why she had picked up the phone to ask Brandt for his blessing to go to class that day. She had been seeking permission to dismiss what she was hearing herself say.

She also realized that she had assigned a meaning to the experience that wasn't actually the lesson. She decided that her child being hurt was evidence that she shouldn't take care of herself, when in actuality, the lesson was to honor herself more—to honor her feelings as warning signs and information.

Many of us are too afraid to follow our intuition or our spirit because it may contradict another's plans, or because we believe others will suffer if we do. Believe me, you will find others who will confirm your fear. However, a healthy relationship is made up of two people, each committed to themselves as being whole and complete, standing side by side with great respect, not obligation to one another.

Mia knew she would continue to suffer in a haze of guilt and codependence until she took a fresh look at herself and what she was

> *Being in partnership,
> not a dependent
> or a codependent,
> creates the best
> likelihood for healthy,
> fulfilling sustainable
> relationships.*

committed to. She saw that she was in a unilateral relationship based on what she gave and did for others, thinking she had chosen a relationship that was based on respect, kindness and partnership. She was trapped in a loveless marriage and staying in it because she was committed to her husband and child.

Ultimately, no relationship is ever really a failure; rather, it is an opportunity to grow, to teach us things about ourselves and the way we learn compassion and forgiveness. Mia and Brandt divorced, and a year later, she is working on forgiving him—and herself—for not knowing then what she knows now. In the meantime, her daughter is getting her master's degree and Mia is going to Paris with—you guessed it—the man of her dreams! Instead of leaving her for how committed she is to her path, her life and herself, he is loving her for it.

SOMETHING'S GOTTA GIVE!

Once, when I was eleven years old, I peeled off one of my favorite shirts, wadded it into a ball and gave it to a friend simply because she mentioned how much she liked it (a trend that continues to this day, except now I layer my clothes).

I could tell she thought I was weird, but I didn't really care: giving it to her made me feel good. What started as an instinctive tendency quickly turned into an identity, and my life as a giver had begun.

By the time I was eighteen years old, I had gleaned an essential truth about living a fulfilling and happy life: it is essential to maintain a generous nature and a sincere desire to serve. About ten years later, I learned the shadow of that lesson: that a generous nature and a sincere desire to serve come with a price.

I had carved out a career by opening the Adolescent Chemical Dependency Unit at my local hospital, and found myself in a position where saying "no" was a luxury I didn't think I could afford. How could I say no to working a double shift at the hospital when my fifteen-year-old patient was dying in the intensive care unit from an overdose of synthetic cocaine? How could I possibly say no to the after-hours call from the mother of an eleven-year-old boy hooked on heroin, whose own father was pimping him out for drugs? At the end of the day, my list was long, filled with people who needed me and what I had to give. Never mind that I had severe anxiety attacks, that I was sleep-deprived and had no life beyond my commitment to serve. I was proud of my strength and my capacity to give.

One blood disease, shot adrenals, and a panic disorder later, I learned the hard way that my physical energy was finite, and I decided to climb off the proverbial cross. I took up yoga and dancing, and spent more leisure time with my family and friends, but it was only after coming face to face with my own needs that I saw things in a different light. I realized that the needs of everyone else were not more important than my own and that to dream of, and desire, a life beyond what I could do for "you" was not self-indulgent or selfish, but necessary for everyone concerned.

At first this was terrifying; I thought I might never get up, or worse, that I might never GIVE again. But it wasn't long before I came to believe the wisdom in the phrase, "You cannot give what you don't have," and learned to trust the following adage:

"The same God that watches over me watches over you."

The next time you find yourself in a position to give, do so—not because you have to, need to, or someone else wants you to; not because you feel guilty or manipulated or are trying to reserve your spot in heaven; but simply because you can. Then ask yourself when you last had a massage, took yourself for a walk, fooled around in your garden, read a trashy novel, or just sat with yourself listening to the beat of your own heart. Take a moment to appreciate the millions of things you have given in this lifetime to get you where you are. Remember to say these words to yourself: "Something's gotta give—to me!"

THE SECOND TOOL: THE MAGNET

While loving yourself as a practice is the first step, being committed to how you express that self-love in all areas of your life and relationships is the next.

If it's commitment you want, give it to yourself first. So many women complain that men can't commit, won't commit—or worse, that they are totally incapable of committing. That's just not true. Men can commit: and can be very discerning about who and what they will commit to, as they should be. The question is, what are you committed to?

There is nothing more attractive than a person who has a strong commitment to themselves and their own path in life. While many men may be attracted to damsels in distress, the healthy man usually chooses a strong, capable partner—someone to stand as an equal by their side. So, don't wait for someone to complete you; be the person you want to attract in relationship.

Like so many women, Mia found it easier to be committed to her path, passions and vision when she was alone. Staying true to oneself in the face of a relationship and family is a whole lot for us to juggle. Loving yourself is usually the first thing to go, if it was ever there in the first place. Being committed to yourself may be something you'll have to fight for.

Being *committed* to yourself is about *how you express* your love outwardly. It's about setting boundaries and knowing your limits. It's about acting on your intuition and being true to yourself. The Magnet is about standing for what you are committed to and how to express and extend yourself in your relationships, and in all the other areas of your life.

The funny thing is that when we *do* set limits and boundaries, when we tell people what we are committed to and are true to ourselves, we are sometimes met with rejection. People may take themselves away. They just up and leave when they don't get what they want. The deeper we get in the relationship—marriage, children, property, retirement accounts, friends, pets and on and on—the more it seems we have too much to lose, so we succumb to *their* needs. We are also manipulated when we believe that we can't live without certain people in our lives.

So, yes, committing to yourself is a difficult step, and a powerful tool and skill to develop. No matter what level of self-esteem you have, this

> *Being sincerely committed to yourself does not mean being insensitive to others' needs.* ♡

tool tests your ability to be true to what you are committed to. Yet in the face of it all, unless we commit to ourselves and realize how important it is to *engage* in a Daily Practice of self-care, we will only continue to attract relationships that are unhealthy and to repeat patterns of self-sabotage and neglect. That creates the same climate, giving us more of what we don't want. A Magnet's job is to attract. The more committed you are to yourself, the more attractive you will be and the more likely you will be to attract someone who supports your commitment.

EXERCISE: IDENTIFY YOUR PATTERNS

You keep doing what you're doing, you get more of what you've got.
—WERNER ERHARD

What's your pattern? Your relationship shtick? Your routine?

The Center for Disease Control and Prevention reports that most women will have an average of four sexual partners in her lifetime. This is likely a conservative number, as many of us are not at all "average" (or not so dishonest!). Even four lovers a year over the course of ten years equals forty intimate partners. It can add up quickly. So the chances of you having or developing a relationship pattern are pretty high. You likely will approach a relationship in a specific way and end a relationship in a certain way. The key is to break free of the unconscious habits that aren't serving you.

> *Being truly committed to yourself and your life's path and purpose is a real man-Magnet.*

A relationship pattern is a way of being in a relationship that is unsatisfying, unhealthy or self-sabotaging. Unconsciousness is defined as *your level of unawareness of who you are and why you do what you do.* So, learn about yourself, become more aware of who you are, what makes you tick, why you are attracted to who you are, and ultimately why you choose the kind of relationships you do.

The following exercise is enlightening and will increase your odds of manifesting a truly healthy, fulfilling, sustainable relationship!

First: You're going to need some lined paper, like a yellow legal pad.

Next: Write (lengthwise), at the top of the page, the names of all your past and present significant relationships. For example:

Ron   Ivan   Shawn

Spread 'em out and give 'em room to breathe! This may be the first time you've looked at them all at once. Be gentle with yourself!

Now, underneath each name, write down what initially attracted you to that person, or what kept you interested. For example:

Ron	Ivan	Shawn
charming	sexy musician	sexy
successful	totally unlike Ron, bad-boy type	sensitive, liked to talk
liked to play golf	great in bed	not so materialistic and liked to wine and dine me
sexy	driven	creative

Next, draw a line underneath what attracted you, and below that, write down the reasons the relationship ended. For example:

Ron	Ivan	Shawn
angry/suppressed	stuffed his feelings	too sensitive
verbally abusive/cruel	hit me	too needy, clingy
superficial	drank too much	drank too much
alcoholic, I think	cheated	pot
cheated	disrespectful	yes man

Your choices say more *about you* than *about the men* that you have picked. Your choices are also part of the transition from external referencing to internal. Notice when the qualities that attracted you were external references, like the way the guy looked or how sexy he was. Just notice. Our patterns started back when we first abandoned our authentic selves on a mission to be loved, when we were just children looking outside of ourselves—primarily to our parents—for validation. We wanted to be seen as we really were. When we were not seen, were rejected or denied, we interpreted that to mean that whoever we were must not have been "enough," even though our parents' behavior likely had nothing to do with us. Consequently, we abandoned our true selves out of survival and began to seek love in ways that have now become our *patterns.* So that's what we are looking for here, clues about our inauthentic behaviors masquerading as our true self. One way to identify them is to look at what you are repetitively drawn to and how most of your relationships end. Notice, in the above example, that all three of these guys were chosen largely for their sexiness. Two of them cheated, and all three abused alcohol or pot. This is a pattern.

Here is what Scarlett, whose story you'll be hearing more fully in the next chapter, initially was attracted to, and what kept her interested in the guys she dated:

Wes	Lear	Maurice	Elden
gorgeous	hot	attorney	very driven
sarcastic	funny	hilarious	entertaining
sexy body	great looking	great body/sexy	sexy
wealthy family	trust fund baby	modeling career	financially secure

Here is a chart of how her relationships ended:

Wes	Lear	Maurice	Elden
cheated	cheated	cheated	cheated
left for roommate	left for her hairdresser	left because he was gay/ only wanted sex anyway	made promises he didn't keep (none of them)

In hindsight, when she looked at her patterns in the above charts, Scarlett could see what these men had in common: they were all self-centered cheaters. When we talked about how her patterns were a reflection of her unconscious childhood wounds, she started to see how she attracted partners to heal those wounds. Scarlett looked even further back, beyond her romantic relationships, and realized that the pattern extended to her mother leaving her for a life with a more exciting man than her father.

She had come to believe that when it comes to love, people leave for selfish reasons. She told herself that something must be wrong with her for them to leave; and she spent most of her time and attention focusing on how to "get" the guy to want her—by having sex early on, and by being accommodating, entertaining and so on, so they would stay. The problem is, this did not work for her, as it rarely does for anyone.

While the relationship pattern is familiar, it is not what we are really wanting. It was not her fault that her mother left, but as children do, she took personally her mother's leaving. Sound familiar? The problem is that beliefs are powerful and can actually cause us to attract that which we do not want. We want to make sure that our beliefs are magnetizing to us that which we do want. Identifying our patterns and beliefs is a first step toward transforming them.

Even if this isn't your exact story, you can probably see how it happens. We try to be what our parents want us to be so that we are bestowed with love. It seems only natural. The problem is, love is nothing to be earned. Rather, it is a reflection of our divine nature and if we do not have parents or people who strongly influence that initial imprinting in the most high, divine way, we do what Scarlett did: we spend our lives trying to figure out who and what we need—outside of us—in order to be loved. Thus, external referencing is born.

During my workshop—when Scarlett began to see that these patterns were not her fault, that she was not bad for choosing these men, that she was only desperately trying to get someone to finally love her as she had never felt loved by her parents—she began to unravel some of the pain that was embedded in each of her stories. And when she really understood that she was trying to get something outside of herself that was not possible to get, she began to look for ways to give that love to herself, first by facing the truth. The journey to internal referencing began as soon as she realized what she had been doing.

The real danger in not facing these unconscious patterns is not only forever repeating them, thus further entrenching ourselves into an inevitable spiral of despair and hopelessness. The real danger is not breaking the cycle of conditional love, thus teaching our children that they, too, must earn our love, and their children must earn their love, and so on. We pass on an impossible legacy that leads to an endless cycle of unconscious pain and suffering. That is, until we make the decision to see our own patterns, to face and heal our past hurts and wounds, and to feel them all the way out loud. Remember, this is what your Daily Practice is for!

But many of us feel we cannot look at ourselves. "It's not us, it's them!" we cry. "If you knew him, you would understand. *I am a victim!*" And, like Scarlett, many of us had every reason to believe we were victims. Our stories are very convincing. But I am asking you to look deeper. Is believing that you are a victim really working for you? Are you free? Do you feel love toward yourself, your body, your soul? Does your spirit sing?

> *There is no **we**
> without **me**.*
> 〇𝓃

Bonus Exercise: The Letting Go Ritual

Now go ahead and set aside a little time for yourself to ritualize letting go of your past, your patterns and the old ways that no longer serve you. While the process of staying awake and growing is ongoing for most of us on a serious path, this letting go ritual is a beautiful and important way to make peace with your past. It allows you to forgive yourself and those with whom you have been involved. Remember that while forgiving and letting go serves and releases those who you have been involved with, the real power of this exercise is what *you* will experience for having done it. When you forgive and let go, you will set yourself free from lingering resentment, be more open to trust and make more room in your heart to love more deeply that which you do want in your life!

Having sat with many different healers over the years, I have adapted the following ceremony, taking a little of this and a little of that into my own intuitive recipe.

You'll need a bowl, some water (preferably blessed), and some sage or incense. Choose a place to go where you feel safe, a place that is sacred to you. It could be in your backyard, at the beach, in the mountains or near your favorite stream—wherever you will feel safe and private. Don't forget matches or a lighter.

IT IS UP TO YOU

You, and only you, hold the key to real freedom and true love. We must see that these patterns are NOT who we are, and that it is not the pattern that we need to change. We need to recognize that who we are is NOT who we have been pretending to be. If we want to know real love we must face this fact, feel the sadness and grief, the hurt and anger and all of the feelings that accompany feeling that we are not enough. Remember, ultimately this exercise will say more about *you* than them, which is the most salient point of this exercise. *We cannot change anyone else; we can only change ourselves.* WHY you pick the patterns is not as important as *becoming aware that you have patterns.*

Regardless of how you got here, the point is to look. Look and see what about you was attracted to the person you chose as a partner. Why did you not inquire further? Why didn't you wait to see if who they were was the same as who you thought they were? What can you learn about yourself from this self-inquiry? What can you learn about how you self-sabotage by picking men who are broken so that you can feel in control, or needed? What led you to make these choices? We need to look and to inquire (not judge!), so that we can learn and heal the underlying causes and wounds, and perhaps choose something healthier and more fulfilling!

Keep in mind that these exercises will help you *learn about you.* They are usually full of surprises, and some may not feel so good! Be gentle with yourself. Looking is an act of self-loving. Doing something different next time is the ultimate act of love!

Then:

1. Make a copy of the pattern process. Put it away for safe-keeping, in case you want to reference or adjust it later.

2. Take the original process with you (whether or not you have decided to copy it).

3. Allow yourself half an hour, at least, and go to this sacred place of yours.

4. When you arrive, sit somewhere comfortable and get grounded. As we discussed in the SHOMI® method in chapter 3, grounded means becoming connected through your body to the earth. Bring your thoughts to a pause and your attention to yourself and your breath. Feel your life force as it connects to the earth beneath you. Notice a pronounced feeling of being connected and solid, "in your body." Close your eyes. Take a few full breaths, and with each breath, drop away from your mind and deeper into your body! Find your relaxed self, your center within. Feel a sense of well-being throughout your body and deep within your belly. Breathe a few more breaths here.

5. Start your ceremony with a prayer, perhaps resting your hands on your lap or in some familiar or sacred prayer pose.

6. Offer your gratitude for all things you are thankful for, *sincerely* grateful for, even the simple things: your ability to draw breath in this moment, to be on the right side of the ground, or whatever else is real for you.

7. Offer your blessings to those who may need them or who are suffering, challenged or ill—and for those who may have harmed you, that they will find peace in their hearts.

8. Ask for guidance for the ritual you are about to perform. Ask for guidance from within to help you find the best and

highest words to speak as you begin to offer your past and cut loose the ties that have bound you to all who no longer serve you, returning both of you back to your highest selves.

9. Sit in silence for another moment or for as long as feels right. Then, open your eyes and fill your bowl with the sacred, blessed water. Next, dig a hole about the size of your fist. Take a deep breath, and find a silent place inside and offer your prayers. Pray for all the relationships you have, and for those you are leaving or want to let go of. Find the words that are appropriate and come naturally to you.

Here are some of my words: *I now release the past old hurts and pain that were inflicted on me, that I inflicted on myself and that I inflicted on these others (fill in the blank). I offer my forgiveness to them and to myself, and I honor them as teachers along my path who helped me grow into the best version of myself. Blessings to us all as I let go, making room for what I am wanting now.*

Make up your own words. They will be perfect!

10. Then light the list on fire (carefully!). Let it burn to ash. Capture the ash in the bowl of water, and pour the water and ash into the hole you dug in the ground. Perhaps you want to place a feather in the ground to complete the ritual and give your offering flight—Godspeed, as it were!

Feel free to make up your own sacred ceremony—maybe incorporating the physical elements of fire, water, earth and air with the spiritual elements of gratitude, blessings, forgiveness and release—in a whole new way that suits you best. Be creative. Have fun with it. Enjoy! The idea is to clean the slate so you can create a fresh beginning. And get ready—the experience is often powerful and palpable!

Chapter Six

The Stud Finder

Love never dies a natural death. It dies because we don't know how to replenish its source. It dies of blindness and errors and betrayals. It dies of illness and wounds; it dies of weariness, of withering, of tarnishing.
—Anaïs Nin

Scarlett was a single mom mending another broken heart, only this time her ego wrote a check that almost cost her life. She and her beloved had traveled—this time with a promise ring in place on her hand—to the sultry sands of Ibiza, where Scarlett could show off her competitive diving skills. "Look at me!" she cooed, diving off the treacherous cliff. But the tide suddenly withdrew, the shallow water not deep enough to catch her, as she plummeted to what was almost certain death.

Her neck fractured in five places, her boyfriend gave her mouth-to-mouth, resuscitating her from death. She was airlifted to the local hospital where, several hours later, she emerged from surgery paralyzed from the neck down, with five metal plates in her back. The doctors said she would never walk again.

For a year she was confined to bed and a wheelchair, enduring bedsores and every other possible hardship you can imagine. Then, with sheer will and determination to walk again, walk again she did. Despite their love for one another (which, in hindsight, was largely sexual chemistry) her boyfriend left her, this time for her hairdresser.

I, too, was a single mom at the time, engaged (technically) to some-one who wasn't an alcoholic (technically). Hooray for me!

At that time enlightenment wasn't being sold online for $24.99; there *was* no online; and if you wanted to wake up, you had a cup of coffee. If you wanted to make a phone call, you pulled over to use a pay phone; and if you had something important to say you mostly did it in person.

Scarlett and I stepped out of the long, glossy limousine—she eagerly, I reluctantly—and entered the crowded meat market at San Francisco's bustling, always happening Triangle area. I knew, the instant we got out of the car, that we were headed for trouble. My girlfriend, brimming with fairy tales and bridled desperation, and I with brimstone and jade. *All is fair in love and war,* I thought. *Somebody bar the door.*

In addition to my mother's "pearls spared for swine" indoctrination ("You'll never meet a good man in a bar"), I knew I had developed my father's gift, a supernatural ability to detect other people's bullshit, in every language ("All men want to do is #&$@! you"). Therefore, for me a bar was a remedial no-fly zone; nothing counted, particularly men. Besides, I, too, had recently been scorned.

The scene was quintessential. Location, location, location. "Excuse me . . . pardon me . . . sorry . . . hey . . . what are you looking at?!" I mut-tered as we walked through the crowd, vying for prime real estate nearest the closest bartender. My girlfriend and I both had only one thing on our minds—love. She to find it, rope it and tame it; I hoped to interro-gate it carefully, curiously and selectively.

"Oh my gawd, do you see that guy?" she yelped, not even trying to be cool about staring or broadcasting her remarks.

I looked without moving my head, "Yeah . . . so? He looks like Keith Partridge or . . . what's his real name? David Cassidy!" I was attempting to gracefully collect my money, napkin, martini glass and beer bottle in the midst of what felt like the running of the bulls. (In my head, I could hear my mother saying, "Ladies don't drink beer," so the fancy glass was my way of compromising.)

"I know him," Scarlett continued. "I think I dated him once! Or maybe . . . wait . . . oh my gawd, he's a CALVIN KLEIN UNDERWEAR MODEL!"

"Calvin Klein model? Uhhh . . . G-A-Y. Next!"

"Come on, he's hot. Let's go talk to him." She trailed off toward Underwear Boy. I followed behind, with morbid curiosity—of course. She waved me over like a trail guide, physically moving a few people to make room for my arrival.

"Maryanne, this is, uhhh, Keith," she said pushing us together as if we should hug. I backed up, trying not to laugh too hard at the thought of him looking like Keith Partridge. More important, I had a two-foot rule, admittedly tough to enforce in a jam-packed bar. Bottom line, I was not a hugger.

"Hey," he slurred gently, offering his hand, the one with his drink in it. Then our inebriated amigo slopped his drink all over my new, black, open-toed, Brazilian suede pumps.

"Harrumph," I grunted. "Gay, drunk—oh, and an idiot! I'm going to the bathroom."

"Come on," she whined, "stay here."

My disdain for arrogance was reflexive, and my repulsion for stupidity was autonomic. Underwear Boy may have been oblivious to my scorn, yet he could not resist ordering an á la carte serving of testicular kabash. Which at the time, funny enough, was my specialty.

And unless you were a drunken, arrogant idiot, one bite was all you needed. As I was contemplating whether or not this fool was worthy of the effort, in walked a six-foot-one cool breeze with perfectly tousled hair; a green-eyed amusement park dressed in a soft, black leather coat. He introduced himself like a gentleman and we engaged in some witty banter. Little did he know he had potentially saved Dumb #&$@!'s life.

"Oh my God, a man who speaks in complete sentences . . . how Cartesian," I lobbed, garbling the last part under my breath. Turns out Bright Eyes was a "friend" of Dumb #&$@!'s. Go figure.

"At your service, Mademoiselle," he volleyed. "Can I get you a drink?"

I leaned my face into my girlfriend's big hair, "Oh my God, a smart, witty… gentleman? Not possible. I must be drunk." She gave me a throaty courtesy giggle, but her attention never left her target. It was plain, however close our physical proximity, that I was on my own.

I didn't care what anyone said, I loved to dance. And when I wanted to dance, it really didn't matter where I was, what I was doing or who was looking. There didn't even have to be music; I could sing in my head. I didn't even need a partner; just given some space I'd start to groove. While Cool Breeze had caught my eye, my mother's *Never meet a man at the bar* admonishment screamed, *Time to go!* in my head. "Come on, let's go," I said, sipping the last of my drink and looking for a place to set it down.

"Why, where we going?"

"I want to dance. Say good-bye."

I had another rule: never leave your sister. *Never!* "Do you guys wanna go dancing?" I heard her say. There was no way she was going to let this guy out of her grip.

The four of us waited for the driver to pull up. "My" guy thought the whole limo thing was ridiculous; "her" guy thought it was cool. I couldn't have cared less, as long as I didn't have to drive.

"How much?" I asked the guy at the door. My guy had a name, Carson. As befits a gentleman, Carson paid for all of us. I didn't like it. Moreover, I didn't like that I liked him, because now a whole other thing was going to happen. What I hated more than anything, I think, was that I was going to have to fight off the horrific sensation of impending vulnerability. I was *not* going to lose control. Stupid girls lose control. Dumb-dumbs fall victim to such contrived patriarchal cultural ritual. Other girls lapped up such nonsense, but not me. No sirree! I had rules, and lots of 'em. If I even thought, for one second, that you were the type of person who could hurt me, I would put my worst foot forward. That usually did the trick.

My girlfriend and I parted company as soon as we entered the club, but it was so small inside that I always knew where she was. Carson seemed mildly interested in the music and easygoing enough to roll with whatever was going to happen. He seemed pretty comfortable in his own skin, which made it even worse. What was I thinking? *Stop thinking*, I thought. *He is a guy; he is the enemy.* There is no such thing as a smart gentleman, and certainly not one comfortable in his own skin. What does that even mean?

I felt like one of those Native Americans who stood on the shore and couldn't see the ships sailing toward them, before their very eyes. Because they had never conceived of ships, they weren't able to see them.

"Oh, no," I said, half laughing, half aghast.

"What?" asked Carson.

We were leaning against the bar watching—the music loud enough to muffle our awkward silence—when I looked over and saw the Shawn guy flipping his hair around like a high school girl. In fact, he was danc-ing like a girl. I couldn't watch.

"What is he doing?" I asked. Carson seemed unconcerned. "He can't be serious, I mean, who does that? Who makes shapes when they dance?"

I was flabbergasted and about to drag my girl off the floor when Carson said, "Look, they're having a good time, so who cares?"

Okay, I thought, *Carson bought them ten more minutes before I have to go run interference.*

"Let's dance," he said.

"Great," I said, thinking, as I would under any circumstance, *Can't wait to see this.*

But he actually surprised me again. He could move, I mean, actually dance. He had rhythm. He wasn't stiff. And I wasn't embarrassed. *That's great*, I thought. *Wait! No, stop thinking that! Who cares if he can dance, he's probably a…a freak or worse than that, he's married and has three kids!*

Next thing I know, I see my girlfriend pressed up against Underwear Boy, smashed into his body in some kind of a lip lock that seemed almost dangerous. I was not then, nor have I ever have been, a voyeur. But this was something else: it was like watching an accident. Back then it was a big deal to see people make out in public. It was almost scandalous. There was no YouTube or Facebook or cybersex. This was a real-life person, desperately wanting another person to want her, to desire her, so she could feel good about herself again—so much so that she would risk being watched by everyone in the room to get her needs met. Two minutes of pulsing chemistry to connect with someone, hoping these precious moments might be a gateway for her dreams. It was almost pornographic. I didn't know if I should call for help or try to change the channel mentally.

All right, that's enough, I thought. *I just can't stand by and watch her dry-hump this guy while he's fishing for her large intestine with his tongue.* Carson didn't flinch when I walked off the floor. I think he may have kept dancing.

"Hi . . ." Tap tap tap. "Excuse me . . . *person.*"

"Uh . . . " Underwear Boy looked up. He had red lipstick smeared around his face. I pointed to a cocktail napkin.

"Yeah, hi. Uhhmm, could I interest you in wiping your face off first before we try and speak?" He took the napkin and wiped his face.

"Right, thank you, that's better. I—rather, *we*—really have to go now. Well, it's been a real pleasure to meet you, and so, that's all."

I looked at my girlfriend, which was almost all I needed to do to clue her in. The "we're leaving" look is an easy one for most people to get.

"'kay, just one sec, I'll be right there," she said with that hormonal flush that leaves you with a permanent silly grin. Carson surmised the party was over and followed me out. I looked over my shoulder as they exchanged numbers and then grabbed one another for one last intestinal plunge.

We were there for two hours, which had seemed like twenty minutes; I always found that so strange when that happened. I offered to drop the guys off at their cars, but they said they didn't mind walking—which meant they weren't done for the night. I was happy to be safe and sound and headed toward bed.

"So, do you think he'll call me?" she asked excitedly.

"Do I think he'll call you?"

"Yeah, I mean, do you think he liked me?"

"Who cares?" I asked, looking out the window. I could feel her disappointment. "Okay . . . I mean, do you really want him to call you?" She looked at me and nodded.

"Wow," I said. "I don't know what to say. Here's a guy who dances like a girl, dresses like he's gay—who probably *is* gay—who flips his hair around like a . . . I don't know what, who clearly would have sex with *anything* that has a hole, who thinks kissing is some kind of tongue-to-tongue combat mission. I mean, come on! Did he find anything in there?"

"In where?"

"In your intestinal wall. I thought maybe he was mining for a kidney, or was trying to steam-clean your lungs. Who kisses like that?"

"What?" she asked.

"What?" I said back, "Really, 'what' is all you have to say?" I was starting to become genuinely annoyed.

Her eyes rolled back and forth searching her brain for an answer. *Ooohh good, a thought making its way to the surface,* I joked with myself.

"So . . . do you think he'll call me?"

I looked at her little face earnestly looking into mine, and let my head fall into my hands. "Do you not hear me? Can you not understand anything I am saying to you? What is it about Mr. Gay-Flash-Dancing-Lizard-Tongue that you are not getting here?"

She too waited for the answer to my question. "First of all, he is probably gay; no, he's absolutely gay. And secondly—come on! He cannot complete whole sentences. Thirdly, he would have sex with *anyone*. I mean, *will* have sex with anyone, and, oh yeah, he dances like an epileptic chicken."

"You're right. I mean he's . . . You're totally right . . . But he's so cute, and… Do you think he'll call me?"

The car slowed as we pulled up in front of her flat. "Get out," I said. "I love you, I do, but get out."

She laughed, as though I was kidding, giving me a big smooch as she climbed over me.

"Whatever you do, *do not* call him!" I yelled out my window into the night as we pulled away.

Of course, she called and called and called him. She absolutely knew his big, mushy lips and Calvin Klein butt were the answers to her prayers, whether he thought so or not. Perhaps flattered by her stalker-like persistence, he eventually called her back. (Turns out he was bisexual, so I was only half wrong). And even though I warned her not to, she got physical with him. So when she came to me in tears—after the fact, of course, when she was desperate to know why he hadn't called her in days—I had to tell her what I thought, again.

"Okay, honey, like I said before, what about who he is seems like such a mystery to you?"

"Well, he was looking at me, and I could tell that look. I know that look. I mean guys who aren't into you, you just know. And he gave me his number, so obviously he wanted me to call. So why didn't he call?"

"Here's the thing, love. He didn't call you for one reason, and only one reason."

"He told me he was working on location in Asia," she said sweetly.

"For six weeks? No, sweetheart. There is only one reason ever in the whole wide world—aside from being abducted by aliens or dismembered in some swift and unfortunate way—why guys don't call, especially after they have gotten what they wanted."

"He's dead!" she said, and started to curl her mouth like she was going to cry.

"Oh Jesus, no, honey, nobody's dead. Stop it! He didn't call because— now here it is, pay attention—*he doesn't want to!*"

She laughed.

"Is this funny? Look, you already have one child because you picked some asshole who left you because he thought being pregnant was the same as being fat. I don't want to

> *"Everything that is subject to arise is subject to cessation."*
> —Buddha

hear it when you show up at my door this time, pregnant with some guy's baby, telling me you didn't know he was gay, an alcoholic, and uninterested in a relationship. Come on, you have been here and done this before—same guy, different name. They are all good-looking, witty, life of the party, have big lips and make you laugh; but, think about it—is this really what you want? Again?"

I vaguely recognized the strange look on her face. (This was before she did the pattern exercise in the previous chapter; in fact, this incident was what led up to her realizing that she needed to do the exercise!)

She looked at me with an intellectually constipated, seriously confused expression. I had seen this look dozens of times before: a kind of wincing consternation mixed with a bereft daze—like you know the truth, but the truth of the truth is just too much to take, so you . . . space out, opt for denial. She was bewitched, she couldn't stand to face the fact that another one bit the dust, that another "not the one" slipped away. She was another year older—none the wiser—and alone, alone, alone some more. She had forgotten the sacred contract her spirit recognized when any two people meet, naked, held in rapture; the promise hinted in each kiss before, during and after. Her soul recognized that she did not use her gift of intuition to choose who to love her and bestow her sacredness upon. It had been overshadowed again by the greedy emptiness she hoped he would fill, longed for him to fill, again and again . . . forever.

Seeing Scarlett compromise herself again and again was like watching reruns of a bad movie I had already seen. Before I woke up and saw my own "stuff" and relationship patterns and tendencies, hers seemed more blatant than my own blind spot. Why would she want to be with someone who clearly didn't want to be with her? Why did she keep torturing herself when he simply wasn't interested in anything but a booty call, the good times, the high times? Why did any of us?

Maybe she had been down this road too many times already, her heart so broken to bits that she was blinded by the pain. Or maybe, like so many of us, she was programmed to believe that love is chemistry and that happiness is somewhere "out there." That if we are enough of whatever someone wants us to be—pretty enough, sexy enough, persistent enough—we will convince someone to love us and live Happily Ever After.

HINDSIGHT: KNOWING WHAT YOU REALLY WANT

Scarlett's story is not uncommon. Many of us think, sure, we know what we want. We have a *type* of person that turns us on (or off) initially. We want athletic, hunky types or brainy, successful businessmen; long-haired, free-spirited, artist types; surfers, bad boys, nerds, intellects, cowboys, adventurers, bikers, and so on. These characteristics are indeed a part of what we may be attracted to; but, just as we have been programmed to look for love outside ourselves, we have also been programmed to believe that love—Prince Charming—comes in a particular package. In Scarlett's case, she liked the types with model good looks who were going somewhere big in life. Beyond that, she didn't think much about it. If they had big juicy lips, a bright future and turned her on, that was enough to pass "Go." That is, until it wasn't.

She, like so many of us, focused on being whatever *he* wanted, trying to win the prize of his attention by being sexy, available, attentive and ultimately giving it up and sharing her sacred sex, thinking that would win his love.

She didn't first consider what his values were, or if he had staying power. She didn't wait to find out if he was a man of his word. Or if he respected women. Or if he was kind, generous, patient, understanding, had good communication skills. Or if he was a one-woman man. She didn't think about what happens when things get tough. *Will he leave? If I get pregnant, does he want children? Does he believe in marriage? Divorce? Does he believe in God? Does he even want to be in a relationship? With me? Now?* These basic questions may have crossed her mind; but instead of asking, she only hoped that he would turn out like Prince Charming—perfect in every way—and would take her off to his castle so they would live Happily Ever After. And because she didn't know what she wanted beyond someone who fit her type and hit her chemistry button, she was not prepared for the excruciatingly painful experiences that came as a result.

Her first love left when she became pregnant. It wasn't only that he didn't want children, he wanted her roommate instead of her. But she didn't know that until it was too late. Her next love left after she became paralyzed, not because she didn't turn him on—she did—but because her hairdresser turned him on more. Again, this pattern revealed itself after the fact, after she had gotten deeply involved.

Many of us think we can't have it all. And believe it or not, we hold men in such little regard (beyond their being hunters and caretakers) that we rationalize their poor relationship skills and don't hold them to a high standard of emotional and moral character. We just chalk their behavior up to a belief that all men are that way, so we have to be the ones to change. We don't see that until we are clear about what we want, we will keep attracting that same level of unconscious behavior, or, at minimum, a man who meets our low expectations.

The endings of Scarlett's relationships devastated her for years, torturing her with questions like *Why did he leave me? What is wrong with me? Why am I not enough?* She tried to get them back, instead of wondering what kind of men she was attracted to, and why, and perhaps choosing someone different next time. But why would she? Isn't chemistry king? Who stops amidst all those sensations? It's like two people running toward each other on the beach in the movies. What woman interrupts THAT to find out what his values are? We fool ourselves into thinking that most men know how to behave and be true, that it only takes the right woman for them to do so. Sound familiar?

Had Scarlett not chosen, ultimately, to look at herself in relationship to the men she chose, she would have continued to pick the same kind of men, ones who screwed her and left her. She would still be feeling that men are to blame for her hurt, and she would likely still harbor intense, buried pain in her heart. Instead, she chose to face her pain, to see how she had chosen men who abandoned her the way her mother did. She realized she had an invitation to heal those old wounds and forgive the men she had blamed for so long as the cause of her heartache. Had she not done her work, she would have remained bitter, unable to trust men, unable to bridge the gap between herself and true love. Instead, she embarked on the journey from being externally referenced to being internally referenced.

THE THIRD TOOL: THE STUD FINDER

The third tool for your Relationship Tool Belt is *knowing what you want*. First, you have to be able to look honestly at what kind of relationships you have attracted so far, *and* to see how your unconscious patterns are standing in the way of creating what you do want in a relationship.

We want a stud—someone who's handsome, tall, strong, accomplished and kind—and then we end up with the same guy we chose last time, with a different name. If we don't take care to sort out and set our intention, we will just keep attracting the same unconscious

> *Love doesn't always look the way you imagine it will.*

patterns from one relationship to the next. Until we face ourselves, commit to ourselves and spend time realizing what it is that we want, we end up either shutting down or telling ourselves bigger lies. We continue to rationalize our choices, feeling further and further detached and estranged from ourselves and everyone else. We begin doing things like choosing relationships that aren't safe; or worse, telling ourselves that *It's just the way it is. All men are dogs so I might as well get used to it.* We marry people we don't love because we think they can't hurt us; we have sex because we are lonely; we stay in relationships because we think that what we want is unrealistic or a fantasy. So we compromise. Eventually we become numb, sometimes sick, gain an unhealthy amount of weight, become workaholics, turn to drugs and alcohol for comfort, etc., all the while wondering how we missed the boat.

It doesn't have to be this way!

A lot of my students right about now start saying things like, "I am not so sure what I want. I just don't want to keep attracting the same kind of guy. What do I do now?"

I tell them, "My hat's off to you, because that's the key we talked about in the first tool! A self-loving posture is to see what we are doing and to see how what we are doing has created what we have had and continue to have."

The Stud Finder will help you define and refine what you want. It takes some reflection, for sure, but every ounce of effort will be rewarded.

Your partner will reflect the amount of care, respect and courage you show yourself. Love doesn't always look the way you imagine it will. It is an inside job, and involves far more than chemistry or appearance. Take care to think deeply about what kind of person you want to get involved with. You are worth it!

So what are you initially attracted to? And how's that working for you so far? Ideally, we do learn from experience. After each failed relationship we tell ourselves, "Wow, I will never get involved with a guy who . . . (fill in the blank) again!" But our memory is short and we get lonely, especially when we see other people hooking up or sharing what looks like the perfect relationship. So we brush ourselves off and try it again . . . and again and again.

> *Getting clear about what we want in a partner helps us end the cycle of attracting relationships that we don't want or that are not healthy for us.*

Rather than attracting another similar, unfulfilling relationship, this time try something different. First, if you're focusing your energy on trying to be the sexiest woman alive to get some guy, you are wasting your time. Most *guyz* (see my definition of boyz, guyz and men at the end of this section) will have sex with almost anyone under the right circumstances. If you don't believe me, ask around. Second, take some time to get clear on what you actually want in a partner. What kind of man do you believe will love and care for you? What kind of values and morals will he have? What is his temperament like? His character? There is no "perfect person," but there IS the perfect person for you.

I understand all too well how easy it is to get involved before you know what you want. Let's face it, it feels so good to be wanted and held—maybe even for the first time in a long while—so you figure, *how bad can it be?* And then you rationalize his behavior:

He'll change once he settles down . . . He's just young . . . When I introduce him to my friends, it will be different . . . He's just used to being single . . . He was that way with her, but I'm different . . . He was going through a phase . . . He has had a run of bad luck.

These are examples of excuses we make for behavior that's unacceptable to us, because we so desperately want to be in love. You also might convince yourself that if he knew who you really are, maybe he wouldn't love you at all. So, you rationalize, what's the big deal if he has a few flaws here and there?

Yes, we all have room to grow, yet there are some obvious things that are worth being clear about from the beginning. Unfortunately, for most of us hindsight prevails yet again. Having foresight and being clear on what we don't want in a relationship is usually where we start if we want to do it differently.

> *Knowing what you want gives you the greatest likelihood for attracting the relationship you have always wanted.*
>
> ℳ

Getting clear about what we want in a partner helps us end the cycle of attracting relationships that we don't want or that are not healthy for us. That's why having a good Stud Finder in your Relationship Tool Belt, along with the Mirror and the Magnet, will help you build the foundation for a healthy relationship by turning your attention inside to yourself—to your heart, your spirit—and to feeding your own soul. You stop the self-defeating, self-destructive behavior by taking care to see what you really do want, and by looking at your relationship patterns.

And there is no need to hurry relationships. The beauty of clarity is that as soon as we know what we want, that clarity and intention sets the universal law of attraction into effortless motion! While all relationships are great breeding grounds for self-realization, learning to identify and name the strengths and characteristics you are looking for in a partner is a powerful and necessary tool. Again, energy flows where attention goes. When you add this awareness to a great practice of self-care and self-love, you set the universal law of attraction into effortless motion.

> *Identifying your relationship patterns helps you to not repeat them!* ⌇

I know, I know, it sounds easy; but knowing what you want isn't always as easy as it sounds. As Scarlett's story points out, if you don't know what you really want, you get more of what you've got—so it is worth every effort you make to get clear.

Since you have already taken a look at your patterns (what you have already gotten) and what you undoubtedly no longer want, we will now explore the power of making a list of what you *do* want in a relationship. Be careful what you ask for—you **will** get it!

BOYZ!

Boy meets girl. ~ Boy wonders what she looks like naked.

Girl says hello. ~ Boy thinks, "She wants me!"

Girl says, "Call me." ~ Boy suspects he could get laid.

Girl says yes to date. ~ Boy brings prophylactic.

Girl agrees to kiss. ~ Boy initiates second base.

Girl agrees to touch. ~ Boy negotiates mounting position.

Girl agrees to submit. ~ Boy is almost done.

Girl wants to snuggle. ~ Boy wants to leave.

Girl wants relationship. ~ Boy wants freedom.

Girl wants commitment. ~ Boy wants to meet another girl.

This scenario is likely an adolescent encounter, one in which neither boy nor girl has realized his or her own worth. But we also see this pattern repeated into adulthood by guyz and gals. Then it looks something like this:

GUYZ!

Guy meets gal. ~ Guy wonders what gal looks like naked.

Gal smiles. ~ Guy knows she wants him.

Gal says "I'll call you." ~ Guy gives her his office voicemail JIC she's a whacker.

Gal initiates meeting. ~ Guy picks Tuesday night for early drinks, JIC.

Gal imagines what their children will look like. ~ Guy hopes she doesn't talk too much.

Gal negotiates sex. ~ Guy rehearses story for optimal quick departure.

Gal calls for days. ~ Guy thinks, "I knew she was a whacker."

Gal is convinced all men are pigs. ~ Guy wonders if she wants to have sex again.

In that scenario the man/boy (looks like a man but acts like a boy) has not yet developed, psychologically or emotionally, much beyond puberty. His aptitude and skills have not matured enough for him to develop sustainable, long-term, mutually satisfying relationships. This unilateral relationship phenomenon is punctuated by his awareness of this fact *and* his unwillingness to tell you so.

MEN!

Man meets a woman. ~ Man wonders what she wants in life.

Woman responds warmly. ~ Man wonders if she is as open and capable as she seems.

Man extends invitation. ~ Woman accepts enthusiastically.

Woman tells man what she wants in life. ~ Man notices they want the same things.

Woman sees man's actions are consistent with his words. ~ Man develops respect.

Man opens his heart. ~ Woman drops her drawers.

Woman speaks her mind. ~ Man tells the truth.

Man and woman wake up and see what they can do to enhance each other's lives!

Wanting sex is natural; wanting to touch, to be close, to be held—natural. As we evolve, however, it is also natural to move beyond narcissism and to include others' feelings and needs into our field of reality. It is a matter of integrity, of value and worth—all concepts that come with emotional and psychological maturity. You become aware that we are on this planet together, on a path of growth. In the meantime, we all need be reminded, now and again, of the difference between boyz and men. Particularly when it comes to creating what we want in a relationship!

EXERCISE:
WRITE YOUR SELF-LOVE PRESCRIPTION

True happiness cannot be found in things that change and pass away.
Pleasure and pain alternate inexorably.
Happiness comes from the self and can be found in the self only.
—SRI NISARGADATTA MAHARAJ

Now you understand that energy flows where attention goes. You have a practice in place for knowing yourself; you have identified your patterns; and you know how to remove obstacles and clear out old emotions from the past so you can see the present more clearly. Let's take a closer look at what it is you would like to attract in a relationship, starting with your relationship with yourself.

While making the list is about getting clear on what you are looking for in a partner, the list will also reveal what you may need to work on in yourself, which will give you further assistance as to how to attract and create a healthy, fulfilling, sustainable relationship. *I LOVE this exercise!*

Since we have already become acquainted with our past patterns, like wanting a hunky, sexy, successful man with big lips and a big…car, I ask you to be as specific as possible about why the qualities on your new list are important to you so you won't have to repeat your old patterns unconsciously. Also take care to notice how you prioritize your list: For example, if you value his looks above all, he will likely mirror that and value yours as his highest priority—and leave if you are not good-looking enough for him. If you value his body, he will value yours. Just remember that whatever you make important about him, he will be a mirror of that priority as it relates to you. (Remember the Big Bad Wolf Exercise!) And, how you value yourself will also reflect what is important to him. This exercise will help you to reveal and release these unconscious Magnets.

The Love Prescription, Part A

First, set aside some time for yourself to sit and reflect on what you're really looking for in a partner. Then, sit down at your computer, or perhaps use lined paper (recycled would be nice), and let yourself go into the world of *all* possibility. Let yourself imagine any and all of the characteristics you are looking for in a partner or relationship. You may want to create sections (physical, spiritual, emotional, etc.) to help organize your thoughts. You also may want to look back at your other relationships and start with some basics. For example:

Physical

- *Preferably at least five feet ten, as I am tall and like being with someone I feel physically safe with*

- *Athletic, but not a fanatic; healthy attitude about exercise*

- *Stocky; butt bigger than mine is ideal*

- *Dark hair preferable but not mandatory*

- *Happy, warm, sincere smile*

- *Healthy teeth*

- *Interested in staying healthy; likes alternative medicine, etc.*

- *Needs hair, on the head! Lots, but not like Jesus!*

- *Clean-cut, but not like Felix Unger, no OCD*

- *Nice hands and feet*

- *Not hairy-bodied, more smooth*

Mental/Psychological

- *Psychologically sound, no history of insanity*

- *Comes from a relatively healthy family*

- *Likes his mother*

- *Likes women*

- *Has healthy male friendships*

- *Committed Relationship is in his top three priorities*

- *No unhealthy addictions like porn, alcohol or drugs, young girls, computer games, etc.*

- *Disciplined*

- *Easygoing*

- *Likes to read and learn*

- *Wants to grow*

- *Has dealt with basic mom /dad issues*

Spiritual/Values

- *Believes in God or The Divine or Great Spirit*

- *Does not have to be religious*

- *Believes in the Golden Rule*

- *Has done a fair amount of work on himself*

- *Generous*

- *Cares about politics*

- *Puts family first*

- *Is loyal*

- *Lives an impeccable life*

- *Has cleaned up his past relationships*

Once you have made your list, revisit it and add layers. You may see that you have forgotten some important things, specific things. For example, one of my students started dating a few months after she took my seminar, and noticed something really odd. She went on three dates in a row with three men named Rich! When she thought about it, she realized that she had put "rich" as one of her desired qualities in a man, thinking that was specific enough. Then she laughed, realizing she had not given any context for the word. It seems the universe has a great sense of humor, and she got what she asked for! As I said earlier in this chapter, be careful what you ask for!

Your basic list is very much a valid list, so not to worry if that is all you come up with. Just keep in mind that should you prefer something more specific, you can easily create that by copying the current list and setting it aside. (We will use it for the next process.) Then, create a more specific list.

Here are a couple of examples:

Psychological Characteristics

He is mentally sound, psychologically balanced and has no clinical issues; he is not dependent on medication for any psychological condition, such as anxiety or depression, or on sleeping pills or the like. The extent of his medicinal arsenal for pain is Advil and maybe some Pepto-Bismol from time to time.

Physical/Body

He takes exceptional care of his body; he makes regular preventative visits to his doctor and dentist, and takes daily measures to ensure his prolonged health. He likes alternative medicine and is curious about new health-care advances, like fish oils and yoga and meditation, but he is not a fanatic. He is curious about the mind/body connection, but not militant about it.

Spiritual

My partner is not necessarily religious, rather he has a personal relationship with God, The Divine or Great Spirit. He believes that developing and deepening a connection to his spirituality is a fundamental and important part of his life.

Try not to leave anything out—let your imagination and heart run wild! You may have several pages when you're done, and that's great. The more detail and emotion, the better.

When I made my own list, I noticed that several of the traits I wanted in a partner, I was *not*—like disciplined or emotionally consistent. I considered myself a free spirit, and my emotions sometimes led me on a roller-coaster ride. I also wanted someone who was financially secure, though I had not yet achieved that. I wanted someone who wasn't afraid of life, while I was terrified of so many things and had spent years struggling with an anxiety disorder! Once I saw this, I had to remind myself that water seeks its own level and that I was not a victim, did not want to be rescued or held hostage. If I wanted a real partnership free of unhealthy dependence, I had more work to do.

I took out my list and circled all the traits that I wanted him to be that I was not. The circled items became my own self-love prescription. After careful review, I used that list as a guide for doing some serious inquiry; and I saw that not only did I need to change some of my beliefs and behaviors if I wanted to attract a healthy, fulfilling partnership, I also had some cleaning up to do from previous relationships.

Wherever possible, I have apologized or made amends in ways that are in integrity. I have an altar where I place the names of people or situations I am conflicted about or feel are not clean, and I pray about them until I feel a clear path of action to make it right. Sometimes contacting the people isn't advisable or may do more harm. In those cases, I pray for peace for them and their families. In other cases the relationship may be too raw and I have to wait. I have made being in integrity with my past a priority, and it has been an important part of my practice. I am happy to say that the list has dwindled and I continue to be as mindful as possible about these matters.

The Love Prescription, Part B

Get a highlighter or a pen and, on a copy of your list, circle or highlight all the qualities or characteristics you listed that you are NOT, or currently don't possess. For example, if you want an athletic man but you're more of a sedentary type, circle the word "athletic"; if you want an outgoing man but you're a bit shy, circle "outgoing"; if you want a rich man but you're struggling to make ends meet, circle "rich." In the example below, I have put in bold the characteristics I wanted in a man but did not fully embody myself!

Physical

- *Preferably at least five feet ten, as I am tall and like being with someone I feel physically safe with*

Athletic, but not a fanatic; healthy attitude about exercise

- *Stocky; butt bigger than mine is ideal*
- *Dark hair preferable but not mandatory*
- *Happy, warm, sincere smile*
- *Healthy teeth*
- *Interested in staying healthy; likes alternative medicine etc*
- *Needs hair, on the head! Lots, but not like Jesus!*
- ***Clean-cut, but not like Felix Unger, no OCD***
- *Nice hands and feet*
- *Not hairy-bodied, more smooth*

Mental/Psychological

- ***Psychologically sound, no history of insanity***
- ***Comes from a relatively healthy family***
- *Likes his mother*
- *Likes women*
- *Has healthy men friends*
- *Committed Relationship is in his top three priorities*
- *No unhealthy addictions like porn, alcohol or drugs, young girls, computer games, etc.*
- ***Disciplined***
- *Easygoing*

- *Likes to read and learn*
- *Wants to grow*
- *Has dealt with basic mom /dad issues*

Spiritual/Values

- *Believes in God or The Divine or Great Spirit*
- *Does not have to be religious*
- *Believes in the Golden Rule*
- *Has done a fair amount of work on himself*
- *Generous*
- *Cares about politics*
- *Puts family first*
- ***Is loyal***
- ***Lives an impeccable life***
- *Has cleaned up his past relationships*

The Love Prescription, Part C

Next, write the qualities or characteristics you circled on another sheet of paper. This new list is what you will use to write what I call your Self-Love Rx! That's right, a prescription for you to take to heart and work on, because remember: *we attract what we believe we are.* If you want a man who offers support, start supporting yourself, and—trust me—so will he! If you want a man who listens, start listening to yourself. If you want wealth, learn about it and start to create it for yourself. The amazing thing is that you will spend less time looking for someone who completes you and more time looking for someone you *want* to be with!

The Love Prescription, Part D

Take each circled or highlighted quality from your list and write an intention or goal based on it. Then write out action steps that you can and will take to give yourself that which you seek in others.

Here is an example of what a Self-Love Rx looks like, using the example from the previous list:

My Self-Love Rx

Original quality that I sought in others: *athletic, but not a fanatic; healthy attitude about exercise*

My intention: I will listen and pay more attention to the overall health of my body.

The action steps I will take to manifest this commitment:

- Move my body four times a week, minimum.
- Put good things in my body 80 percent of the time (20 percent is allowed for some treats).
- Tell myself positive, loving things about my body.
- Sit in silence with myself (honoring my new body-centered practice).

Original quality that I sought in others: *Clean-cut, but not like Felix Unger, no OCD*

My intention: I will be more relaxed about my appearance and not hold myself to such self-defeating pictures of perfection. I will approach my appearance from a place of fun and celebration, rather than from criticism and judgment.

The action steps I will take to manifest this commitment:

- Cover my mirrors for one week and see what happens.
- Journal what some of my fears are about being unattractive.
- Wear some things that are "wrong" or fun instead of appropriate.
- Focus more on my feeling state than how I appear.

- Surround myself with supportive, unconditionally loving people as I learn to unconditionally love myself.

Original quality that I sought in others: *Psychologically sound, no history of insanity.*

My intention: I will continue to develop skills that help me stay mentally and psychologically balanced.

The action steps I will take to manifest my commitment are:

- Take yoga classes that help me with staying present, breathing and meditating so that I experience a greater degree of peace.
- Hang around with more psychologically and emotionally balanced people.
- Read and listen to personal development material, replacing negative thought patterns with new, more self-loving thoughts, rather than watching TV or numbing out.
- Continue with the SHOMI® method and listen to whatever feelings may need to be expressed so I can stay current and present with what's happening now.

Original quality that I sought in others:

Comes from a relatively healthy family.

My intention: I will heal my relationship with my family of origin (those past and still alive) starting with me.

The action steps I will take to manifest my commitment:

- Learn what my healthy boundaries are and draw those lines when necessary and appropriate.
- Develop my compassion and understanding by remembering that we all have issues and are struggling to seek freedom of being, and that there are many paths up the mountain.
- Be mindful of my responsible-communication skills.

- Continue to pray for guidance, revealing the high road, whenever possible.
- Clean up my part of the story (what I did to create any discord or pain) in those relationships, whenever possible.
- Remember that just because I am uncomfortable doesn't mean anything is wrong.
- Keep a journal to empty myself of any intense feelings better expressed in private.

Original quality that I sought in others: *Disciplined*
My intention: I will develop more discipline in my life by changing how and where I focus my attention.
The action steps I will take to manifest my commitment:
- Choose to think through to the consequences of trivial or frivolous choices about how I spend my time.
- Get back on the horse as soon as I realize I have fallen off.
- Choose some achievable goals and take action toward them (list those goals here).
- Study people I believe have achieved the kind of balanced success I admire, and adopt some of their habits!
- Surround myself with people who do what they set out to do rather than just talk about it!

You will see that singling out the characteristics on your wish list that are not your strengths offers you a prime opportunity to develop these abilities for yourself. This exercise will give you more self-esteem and a greater feeling of self-worth, which is absolutely magnetizing and fulfilling.

Now, keep your list posted where you can see it, and follow your prescription! For years, I've had Self-Love Rx's and reminders for myself written on sticky notes and construction paper taped up in my bathroom, office and bedroom. Again, energy flows where attention goes!

BONUS EXERCISE: DEAL BREAKERS

Now that you have identified some of your most self-sabotaging, self-defeating patterns and have created a self-esteem-building, beautiful Self-Love Rx, let's create a list of your non-negotiable issues to help you stay the course.

A non-negotiable is some behavior or characteristic that would stop you from entering into a relationship with someone, or a reason that would justify ending the relationship. I call that a deal breaker—something you will not accept in your life, or something you cannot live without (such as children, in some cases). Let me ask again: When do you want to know that someone is a pathological liar, is married already, is a con artist, is addicted to drugs or is wanted by the law—before or after you have sex and fall in love?

Choosing someone with these blemishes, let's call them, or less-than-desirable characteristics, isn't always an accident: many of us see the red flags and *move in anyway*. Sometimes we have the belief that we can get the other person to change something that we don't like. We know what we want and what we don't want, but we have some underlying belief that if we are (fill in the blank) enough, they will love us enough and change their behavior. Consequently, we make the mistake of choosing partners who have qualities that are deal breakers, thinking that they will change. Sometimes, we even use their willingness to change as some sort of litmus test for their love: If he *really* loves me, he will (fill in the blank).

> *When do you want to know that someone is a pathological liar, is married already, is a con artist, is addicted to drugs or is wanted by the law—before or after you have sex and fall in love?*

Just the other day my 88-year-old mother-in-law, married for sixty-five years, answered a few questions for me. I asked, "Mom, looking back, if you could have done something different, what would that have been?"

"Well," she said, thinking about her husband, "he always wanted to go hunting by himself every year, and I hated that. For years we fought about it."

> *We do what we do*
> *until we don't.*
> ⟨ᴍ

"But you knew he liked hunting before you married him, right?"

"Yes, but I thought that after a while, I could change him."

This is such a common scenario, the modern version of which is the belief that if I give him what he wants (usually sex) or if I become how he wants me to be, then I will be able to change him. How far from the truth that is! When I really got honest with myself, I could see that I sometimes chose people with the very qualities I didn't want, either because I felt familiar with the unhealthy behavior (e.g: I grew up around alcoholics so I often chose them—a pattern), or because I believed that my intellect or my psychological proficiency was superior. I believed that because I was smarter than they were, they would not be able to hurt me and hence I would be in control.

Putting yourself out there, no matter what, usually makes you feel vulnerable, to some degree. The difference now (if you have been doing the exercises throughout this book) is that you have *you* and a powerful, effective *tool belt* to help you navigate the confusing, scary, emotional terrain that relationships can be!

Of course there is no need to beat yourself up for having ever settled (or for falling in the hole again); we do what we do until we don't. I am saying that it feels like heaven when you have attracted someone who is truly loving, caring, open and capable of a healthy relationship—someone who sees who you really are, who "gets" you and wakes up every day wondering what he can do to make your life better!

Sound too good to be true? Try it! That's right, you have YOU and a direct line to The Divine inside your body, any time you need it. And when you meet someone who's a great fit, you'll know better what choices to make and how to proceed, and you honestly won't believe you ever settled for anything else.

Get a pen and start that list of non-negotiables. They will help you stay mindful of what you do want in your life, and help you to steer clear of what you don't. Here are examples of some issues that you may not be willing to negotiate:

- I want children
- I don't want any more children
- I don't want to be a stepmother
- No drug addicts
- No alcoholics
- No workaholics
- No abuse—verbal or physical
- No porn addicts
- No sex addicts
- No younger men
- No men over 30 (or 40, 50, 60, 70 . . . ?)
- No men with STDs

Be specific, and don't be afraid to personalize the list to match exactly what you can't stand or can't live without. Maybe you have to be with someone who has a certain type of hands or hygiene or religious beliefs. It doesn't matter; it's your list. The point is to know where you are not willing to compromise! Keep in mind that "non-negotiables" are the really important issues, not just the "It would be nice if he had dark hair" preferences that we covered extensively earlier in this chapter, when you made your initial list.

You may want to revisit your first list and make sure you state these items in the positive, so you have a greater likelihood of attracting someone who has the qualities you want, not the ones you don't! For instance, rather than "No sex addicts," you would describe your non-negotiable from the perspective of what you do want: "Has a healthy sexuality that is playful, fun and romantic. Our libidos are perfectly matched so that we both feel satisfied."

Have fun with this exercise, but remember: your life could depend on honoring your wisdom here!

And ladies, hang on to your list—carry it in your purse, staple it to your headboard, put it on your altar—because it's sooo easy to fall asleep when that chemistry kicks in! You never know where or when you'll most need the list. Hey, you may need to attach it with a safety pin to your undies!

Chapter Seven

The Flashlight

The attainment of wisdom is slow and painful,
and few are willing to relinquish familiar views…
—DAVID R. HAWKINS

A fetching, blue-eyed doe with legs for days, Keily, a longtime family friend, had been turning heads since she could walk. She escaped *her* family at eighteen by marrying—surprise!—someone a lot like her mother (and almost as abusive). Keily had three children and spent the better part of eighteen years in an emotionally abusive marriage, which ended finally in a long and ugly divorce that forced her into the work world for the first time.

With her kids almost grown, she bucked up and joined the ranks of gals who flew the friendly skies. Shortly after getting her wings, she found herself grounded with a disabling bout of depression that would last for a decade. She didn't know who she was—a mother? an ex-wife? a flight attendant?—or where she was going, so she concluded that what she needed was another man.

Not having yet met my husband, I still occasionally enjoyed the ritual of getting dolled up and going out dancing in the city. Keily and I, bonded by our past, yet ten years apart in age, were kindred spirits. We had great affection for each other and we both loved to dance. However, despite the fact that she was older, whenever we went out I felt like I was her older sister and she was my reluctant apprentice.

"Am I gorgeous?" she asked, with a blend of insecurity and self-denigration so potent it almost always made me cringe.

"Of course you are, look at you!" I grabbed her by her beautiful, shiny, broad shoulders (one of her best features) and shuttled her in front of the full-length mirror. I was no longer irritated but determined for her to see what I saw: a woman who most other women would *kill* to look like. I knew that Keily's wound-ology was so pronounced she wasn't aware of her beauty, inside or out; she was only obsessively aware of what she believed were her flaws. Having had twins, she thought the mirror mocked her every time she looked in it.

"Come on, you're stunning, let's go!" I said affirmatively, looking for my evening bag. I knew that the longer we stayed fussing with ourselves, the more likely she was to slide into a dark place that would haunt us all night.

"I want you to meet Murphy," she confessed as we shimmied our way down the second flight of stairs inside her apartment building.

"Murphy, huh? Aren't we Little Miss Secretive?" She didn't respond. I knew something was up. For some reason, I had never heard about this person before; for some reason, she had kept him a secret. "So when do I get to meet him?"

"Tonight," she answered coyly.

"Oh, really?"

She seemed instantly confident and sexy when she saw him, the contrast of her milky white skin highlighting his honey brown complexion. He greeted us professionally, a kiss on the cheek for her and a polite handshake for me. Aside from the fact it was almost midnight, I was suspicious, given Keily's level of restrained responsiveness the longer he was with us. Something didn't feel right.

"So, Murphy, what do you do?" I asked, confident that his insincere kiss-kiss greeting was as fake as he was. I went right for the jugular.

"Currently, I am in Public Relations," he said silkily.

"Public Relations? What do you mean, give me an example?"

"Well, right now we are promoting a revolving dance club," he said, looking at Keily. Coincidentally, at that very moment we were standing in front of one such popular "revolving dance club." We were lingering next to the corner where the line was still a block long.

"Oh, you mean like a rave?" I asked, challenging him, because I smelled BS without a doubt. He did not meet my penetrating gaze. Abruptly, he excused himself to shake hands and kiss-kiss a few VIPs walking by, escorting them to the front of the line himself. He exchanged words with the keeper of the velvet gate and then returned to us.

My gaze hadn't changed, as if to say *and you were saying, before we were so rudely interrupted?* "Sorry about that," he said, and then, suddenly nervous, he averted more of my questions. "Ladies, would you like to go in?" He waved Keily over and practically herded us into the building, pulling Keily aside to give her what looked like a bit of a tongue-lashing. Then he disappeared without saying good-bye, which was more consistent with his dubiously polite greeting. Things were starting to make more sense.

"What was that all about?" I asked.

"He's working," she said in his defense.

"Huh, so is that why he met us so late?"

"He's having trouble with one of his partners," she said, not telling herself or me the truth, avoiding my direct question, making excuses for his slightly bizarre and rude behavior. She would be doing all these things a lot over the next eight years.

Close to 2:00 a.m., Murphy mysteriously appeared out of the crowd to join us. We had met some friends inside, and Murphy escorted the group of us across the street to our cars. I made my way to Murphy's side and whispered, "If you hurt her, you will have to deal with me...got it?" I looked into his face to make sure it registered. He smiled. He knew I knew exactly who he was *not*, nor would ever be—Keily's boyfriend. It was the first and last time I saw him hold and kiss her in public.

It wasn't long before Keily had become a great escape artist when it came to Murphy. A crisis would hit, and she would hide in shame because she knew I was not supportive of their relationship, which amounted, in my opinion, to one that subsisted almost solely on booty call.

After he was done doing whatever with whomever, he would call her and come over, have sex and then leave before the sun came up—except when he needed money; and then they would spend hours together "making up" (on the phone, of course). Murphy, using Keily as a sounding board, would whine about his plight in life, how he couldn't catch a break, etc., etc. Keily would then try to express her needs, which—he would remind her—was not the point of the conversation (he was). He would then ask to borrow her "two cents" in the form of hundred-dollar bills.

One of her wishes was that he take her out in public, at least for her birthday, which he had missed for the last few years. He made it up to her by taking her for a drive in his convertible on a Sunday at midnight. When she asked if they could also go out *before* midnight in the city where they lived, he reminded her that he needed to work, and said she was being unreasonable and selfish.

By year four of their relationship, Keily had emptied all her life savings, *loaning* it to Murphy, whose hard times seemed to be an epidemic that followed him at the end of every month. She found out that he was sleeping with three women, including her. Hoping to prove her worth and how much she loved him, she decided to be the one out of his three bed partners who would win him in the end because she would place no demands on him. She would not be jealous, and she would offer him what he really needed: unconditional love, and unlimited access to her body and finances. She told herself that, eventually, he would see the light and choose her. And then they would live Happily Ever After. She loved him that much.

Keily hadn't bothered to ask Murphy if he was seeing anyone else when they first met. She assumed he wasn't, because "why else would he be spending time flirting with me?" She didn't ask if he had ever been married or wanted children, given that she was twelve years older than he and had had a hysterectomy. She didn't want to know if he wanted to be in a committed relationship (which she did), nor did she interview him to see if he was even remotely capable of one. She didn't take care to see if he was a man of integrity, either. She didn't wait and watch to see if what he said matched up with what he did. She was too busy trying to sell herself to Murphy, to win his affection, to get him to love her; too busy trying to be what she thought he wanted her to be, rather than interviewing him to see if he was the kind of man she wanted to invest herself in. Keily was overlooking all the obvious red flags.

Two weeks had passed when she called, hysterical.

"Keily . . . Keily . . . calm down, honey, tell me what happened."

"I got my cell phone bill today."

"And?"

"And it's for $230.00!"

"What am I missing?"

"I lent Murphy my cell phone—and about every two minutes, all last month, I can see it right here . . . Right before and after we would be together, he was calling her," she cried. "And on *my* phone!"

"Who's 'her,' honey? Fill me in."

"She called me and wrote me an email, and God, she is so disgusting. She told me to stay away from Murphy, and she said that I was just his old, fat booty call and an embarrassment . . ." She began sobbing.

I settled back in my chair and, as lovingly as possible, listened to her cry until she could finally catch her breath.

"I am so sick of it," she said. I wished she were sick enough to let go. I couldn't imagine how much more she would take.

"Keily . . . listen to me. What do I always say? What do liars do? Remember, they lie, right?" I wanted her to refocus, to move from being a victim to seeing what was so.

"Right, liars lie," she said halfheartedly.

"Murphy lies and lies. It's what he does, so this is consistent with his behavior. Right?"

"Right," she said, unconvincingly.

"The real question, honey, is that if you know this, why do you put up with it?"

> *You don't ever need to put yourself in harm's way to love or be loved.*
>
> ℳ

And then she said it out loud, something I never thought I would hear. Until she saw it for herself, it wouldn't have done much good for me to point it out.

"Because I kept telling myself that if I could get him to love me, then I must be lovable. Because look what he would have given up to be with me," she said at last, and then began to sob for what might have been five whole minutes. I felt privileged to wait. What a truth she had revealed to herself.

Keily attended one of my seminars toward what turned out to be the end of her relationship with Murphy. She learned that in pointing the finger at Murphy—blaming his withholding love from her, his infidelities, his lies and so on as the cause of her pain—she was being externally referenced. Trying to get love outside of herself, from him or anywhere, was a major source of her suffering. She also had a major "Aha!" moment when she realized the truth: that how she felt about herself directly affected how Murphy treated her; that to the degree she disrespected herself, so did Murphy; that to the degree she devalued her sexuality and felt ashamed of herself, Murphy was ashamed of her too; that to the extent she didn't value her time, neither did Murphy.

As though that weren't enough, she was blown away when she realized that it had never occurred to her to see what *he* was bringing to the table. She had never interviewed him well enough to see if this was a person worthy of her affection, of sharing her bed and her most sacred self with. She didn't even know if he was someone with whom she shared the same values and morals.

In less than three minutes after I first met Murphy, I had guessed that Keily was sleeping with him already, given their intense exchange and her confident sexy posturing. I also guessed that he was hiding something: another woman. In this case, I really hated being right. Keily had decided to overlook the obvious cues and "take the good with the bad." She was in love with him, she said, and it would unfortunately take her eight pain-filled years to realize he was not, nor had he ever been, in love with her.

Ultimately, Keily realized that focusing her attention on herself, attending to her own needs, was the place to start. Learning how to love and respect herself would be her best investment of time, no matter how much she may have thought she loved him. She learned that just because you "love" someone doesn't mean they are a good or healthy choice as a person to be in a relationship with. Learning this was an invaluable act of self-love and self-respect.

This is also an example of why you need to develop mature love, and an imperative lesson: you don't ever need to put yourself in harm's way to love or be loved. In fact, if you are being harmed, it isn't really love that you are receiving. And in the end, Keily realized that she would rather be alone than be treated so poorly by anyone ever again!

HINDSIGHT:
INTERVIEW WELL IN THE BEGINNING

When do we want to know if the man we've just had sex with is married? Or has three children or a sexually transmitted disease? Or is a die-hard bachelor seeing nine other women? Or is gay (most of the time) and really wants men? Or is wanted by the FBI? Keily's story reminds us that sometimes we are so desperate to be loved that we forget to—or just plain don't—ask the important questions because we are busy trying to "get the guy." A veritable recipe for disaster!

Keily's story also illustrates that chemistry is not love; it is merely a hormonal litmus test, not a real indicator of someone's capacity or availability for a healthy relationship. Just because someone wants to have sex with you—or they make you feel good, or they are sexy, or they turn you on—doesn't mean they love you or even want to be in a relationship with you. It doesn't mean that they are a good choice in a partner or capable of being in a healthy, fulfilling relationship. Keily was deeply entrenched in the belief that chemistry is king and that the sexiest woman wins the man. She didn't understand the truth, which is that the sexiest one gets the *sex*, not necessarily the *man*! And she may not be the only one getting the sex—the less sexy ones may be getting the sex, as well. Remember, you get what you put out.

In the long run, being sexually intimate before you really know who someone is can wreak havoc on you. Such a sacred act without real respect, tenderness and boundaries leaves us feeling used, empty and ultimately alone. You deserve more than that, so take care and add your intuition to that emotion. See what kind of choices you will make then. Likely, you'll experience a whole lot less heartbreak and a whole lot more self-esteem and self-respect.

By letting her hormones choose a potential mate and by not listening to her intuition, which is always there to guide us and help us make good choices, Keily put her heart, body and soul in danger of being hurt. She expected this person to give her something he wasn't capable of or willing to give.

The average woman will have several sexual partners in her lifetime. Whether you consider yourself to be above or below average, sharing your sacred self with another human being is one of the most precious acts of intimacy there is. The problem is that most of us are addicted to the juice, the buzz—to being wanted and desired. The high feels so good, we simply can't or won't consider giving it up. It's so intoxicating that we overlook all the red flags and go for the juice, and hope everything will work out in the end. We throw caution, and our precious time, to the wind without thinking it through.

Several months after coming to my workshop, Keily had this to report: She had been carefully practicing her tools, focusing primarily on falling in love with, and loving, herself—a concept that she realized had been foreign to her. She was committed to changing; she didn't want to attract any more of what she had already attracted. Then, a "friend" called out of the blue, ten years after they had last had sex. At that time, he had showed up on her doorstep with a nine-month-old baby, to explain where he had been the previous nine months. He wanted to catch up. She admitted, in hindsight, that her first mistake was that she agreed to meet him. She confessed that she was curious and, well, human. I grimaced—but then I remembered my own trail of relationship horror and despair, and was immediately filled with compassion.

The first red flag came to her attention while they were on the phone. She noticed that while *he* had been the one who called, obviously wanting something, *she* was the one making all the fuss trying to accommodate him. She had offered to come to his neck of the woods, asked if she should pick the place to meet and so on, while he was willing to let her do all the work. Then she stopped in midsentence, reneged and suggested he come to her instead. *She caught herself and did something different*, very different for Keily the accommodator! She had him pick her up. We laughed and decided she got three stars for that alone.

He picked her up a few days later and they went to a little wine bar in her neighborhood, close enough to home that she felt comfortable walking should she want an escape plan. She took this opportunity to "interview" him in a way she hadn't years before when they had dated. It turned out he still was in a relationship with the mother of the baby he proudly presented at her door ten years earlier, and that he was feeling so stressed about their relationship that he decided to call Keily for some comfort. Which, when she did the math, meant he was not only insulting his baby's mother, he was insulting Keily . . . again.

Adding insult to injury, he had the audacity to ask her for a favor. "Baby, I am so tired and stressed out about things lately and was wondering . . . Well, I was wondering if we could go back to your place and have sex." He took a sip of wine and waited seriously for a response.

Keily said the first thing she thought was, *What a cheap asshole, he isn't even offering to take me to dinner first!* This represented more growth: in the past she would have been happy the man took her out in public. Then she felt enraged. "I'd like to go home now."

"Does that mean you *do* want to have sex with me?" he responded hopefully.

She couldn't say why she let him drive her home at that point; she called it morbid curiosity. He neared her house and, instead of pulling in front to let her out, started to park the car. She said, "Look, Joe, I am going upstairs . . . *alone!*" And she got out of the car. He followed her to the door and said, "Come on now, I'm serious, let me ask you a couple of questions." He leaned one of his arms up over her head, posturing himself.

"If your first question has anything to do with sex, Joe, the answer is no. And regardless of what the other questions are, the answer is *no* to them, too. Good night." And she walked inside, closing the door in his face.

I was upset after Keily told me this story, feeling protective of her, as I do for all women who have fought for scraps of love wherever they can get it. I wanted to give him a spinning back-kick, and then quickly realized this was not only illegal but also not very spiritual. *Cancel that,* I thought, trying to practice nonviolent communication (that's in another book, another tool). So instead, I said the other thing I was thinking, "Good for you, I am so proud. You must have felt so good about yourself!"

She beamed, because she was and she did! She told me she had learned two things from my seminar that changed her life forever. The first was the concept of interviewing well. The other was recognizing that trying to get a man to love her or listen to her or hear her or see her gifts was an act of vanity, when she had not yet given those things to herself. For her, this was a major revelation. My hat is off to Keily. She is a lovely lady and an inspiration to us all.

THE FOURTH TOOL: THE FLASHLIGHT

We need to take a closer look, with Flashlights glaring, at what we are getting ourselves into. We talked about knowing what we want; we also need to be able to identify it when it shows up. We need to learn to be discerning and love ourselves enough not to simply take people at face value, but to inquire—especially if we are considering becoming physically intimate.

Ask yourself, when do *you* want to find out if the person you are attracted to, and are considering being in a relationship with is: married, involved with someone else, a lot of someone elses, doesn't want to be in a relationship, is only interested in having sex, never wants children, already has children, is incapable of being faithful, has an STD, is out on bail, shoots heroin, smokes a little crack, thinks nothing of smacking a woman around, has a police rap sheet as long as his johnson, is a member of the KKK or Al Qaeda, has killed someone, is wanted for tax evasion, has never paid child support, and so on! Do you want to know before or after you have sex with him?

At some point, the age-old adage, *Burn me once, shame on you; burn me twice, shame on me*, really applies. In today's world, interviewing well is a MUST! The challenge is, most of us use the hormonal litmus test instead of asking the important questions. When we associate "feeling good" with a certain person, it clouds our ability to see clearly who that person really is; and that's when we get into all kinds of trouble. Even when we love ourselves, are committed to our path and know what we want, sometimes it still takes kissing a few toads before we find our prince. Know that it is highly likely that if it walks like a rat, talks like a rat, and looks like a rat . . . it's almost always a rat!

The Flashlight is a critical tool for your Relationship Tool Belt, as it will remind you of the following:

- Slow down. Love does NOT have a shelf life.

- Chemistry is NOT love. Don't let chemistry dictate where this relationship is going.

- Inquire. Don't be afraid to ask the important questions like, *Are you seeing anyone? Are you married? Do you want to be in a committed relationship? Do you want or have children?* These are not things you want to find out later. It is quite painful to find out the person you have become intimate with does not feel the same way as you feel about them, or is in a relationship with someone else already.

- Watch. Make sure this person's actions consistently match his words. This indicates integrity.

- Love yourself enough to find out who you are with. It takes practice to not let chemistry be your judge, but it will be worth the wait! For most of us, the physical part of the relationship is the easy part.

- Use your Flashlight to look inward for validation and love!

REMEMBER, chemistry is not love, and sex is not a good indicator of someone's capacity for a healthy relationship! Chemistry, while important for most of us, is not enough to sustain a relationship, nor is it an indicator of another person's emotional aptitude or relationship skills.

EXERCISE: ASK THE CRITICAL QUESTIONS

There are only two mistakes one can
make along the road to truth
1) not going all the way, and 2) not starting.
—BUDDHA

Now that we have a complete list of your non-negotiables, here is how we put that list to use: we ask the tough questions. They say the devil is in the details, which explains why so many of us have experienced a kind of hell when it comes to relationship. For some of us, it is terrifying to ask even the most basic questions. We want to know if someone is married, don't we? Or maybe we think it's easier if we don't know! This kind of thinking is what ultimately causes us and others pain, so courage is what is required now. Having the courage to respect ourselves "out loud," and taking care to make sure that people are who they say they are, is not only smart, but a self-loving act.

Keily's story shows us how important it is to ask the important questions *before* you drop your drawers. It also illustrates what can happen when you miss the obvious cues that would have told you that someone isn't who you thought they were. Yes, it can be quite uncomfortable to ask these important questions. You may be afraid of disturbing the delicate chemistry of a new relationship, of turning off someone. Or maybe you have your own secrets or are afraid the other person will ask the same questions of you. Who do you think you are?

First, you are someone who is committed to being the best version of yourself, who is bringing the sacredness back to sex and a relationship—someone who is worthy of a loving, fulfilling relationship. While you may not be perfect, you have every right to inquire into the character and nature of someone who you may choose to share your precious, sacred self with. If someone is that easily turned off or offended, they probably are not living in integrity. OR, they are simply not worth trying to *turn on* in the first place. With all due respect, they may not yet be on a path of growth themselves, nor committed to their highest impeccable selves. Which, by the way, IS NOT an invitation for you to become their teacher or guru (careful here!). Your job, right now, is to interview well and choose wisely.

Let me share a personal story. When my father married my mother, he had just been accused of rape. He took his young, naïve bride to court with him after convincing her that he had been set up. Yet he wasn't listed as a sex offender until years later. Thirty years later, in fact. My father went to jail for molesting my young cousin, who later killed herself as a result of his actions. What I am saying is, my mother would have never thought to ask, never mind believe, the man she loved and had just married could or would ever commit such a heinous act. The list of things we need to know is longer than we think, and sometimes it takes time to find out. Often, though, we simply need to ask or even notice. Sometimes the truth is right under our nose, but because we don't like the smell, we ignore it or deny it.

Sure, it feels good to connect; but once we are loaded up with chemicals in our brain, we are one hundred times less likely to ask the questions and more likely to rationalize the obvious, as my mother did. Uh, like my father was on trial for RAPE. So, as I already said, while it is very important that you ask, also make sure to pay attention to what you discover!

After the suggested questions, I share how you might engage someone into these conversations gracefully, in case you are inclined to space out or get nervous and go blank when it comes down to it. A little rehearsal never hurt anyone. Keep in mind that while you are asking these questions, someone may ask these very same questions of you. Consequently, it would be wise to consider your own answers, as well.

What You Need to Know Before You Drop Your Drawers!

Following is a list of questions that you want to make sure to ask, ones that will support or add to your non-negotiable list. The more specific the questions, the better. Feel free to add to the list based on your own deal breakers. Pass the wisdom on. As you know from a previous chapter in this book, we have lost some of our beloved sisters because they perhaps did not have the courage to ask. And be sure to pay attention to what you hear and see.

- **Are you married?**
  Don't ignore this one; it can be lethal! So many of us pass this one up because we think, *Why would he be flirting with me if he's married?* Or, we don't want to know, because we are so desperate for attention or love that we will take it wherever we can get it. This question, if not asked, will almost always be a cause of great pain, usually yours (and his spouse's)! If he is married, please, please, please don't fool yourself into thinking you can change this reality. If he is really going to get divorced, let him do so and *then* give you a call.

- **Are you currently involved in a relationship or seeing anyone?**
  Now, you may say, "What if he's lying?" Good question. How do we know? This is why I recommend not getting physical until you find out if what this person says and what they do match up. Everywhere—at work, with his

family, friends—it all has to make sense. You want to be sure he is living in integrity to a great degree, so you don't get so attached that you become blinded to his character! None of us is perfect, but some things are just plain non-negotiable.

- **Do you want a real, lasting relationship (or do you just want sex)?**
  This is a GREAT question; and, boy, how many times do we have to get burned before we find this out *before* we get physically intimate? So many of us fall for the chemistry, for being wined and dined like Keily was, only to find out he is with you for one reason . . . sex. Yes, it feels so good to get attention from someone we find attractive, oh yes, yes, yes! Some of us live for it. And in the first five minutes, we are busy fantasizing about our life together, how many kids we will have, where we might live, what we will write on our epitaphs . . . we get carried away. Wow, all that chemistry! It's like a drug, isn't it? We get weak in the knees, a dry mouth and a throbbing heart. Funny—these same feelings course through our bodies when we have a near miss on the freeway or run into a bear in the middle of the woods. But these are just feelings, and they will pass, so think it through.

  Ask this same tough question *of yourself* before you drop your drawers. And ask more questions: Will he respect you in the morning, ask you to marry him, and live Happily Ever After with you? How will you know, if you barely know him (and how will you know if you *want* him to marry you?). Why, oh why, would you leave the answers to these questions to chance?

Okay, maybe you only want casual sex yourself (in my experience, this comprises a miniscule percentage of women on the planet, if they are honest with themselves). Regardless of what you ultimately want, it still pays to ask the questions. What if all you want is casual sex and he wants Happily Ever After? Not to know is still a recipe for disaster. Be honest with yourself. Take care to ask before you get involved and perhaps have your heart broken—or before you break someone else's heart!

- **Do you believe in God or some power greater than yourself?**
  This is a question that made all the difference for me, and the answer that told me volumes about someone. In hindsight, the ones who did not believe in God or have some spiritual connection truly did the most damage in any relationship—to themselves, and in life in general. It is not a foolproof question, but it can tell you whether someone has a perspective on the greater reality: that they are not the center of the universe. Also that they feel a sense of responsibility to behave in alignment with their moral code! A hard question to ask, maybe; but critical. This is one of the most important questions I learned to ask!

For some people it is enough just to know that the other has a belief in a greater power, but for others it may be important that you share the same religion. Be really honest with yourself about what is actually important to you, and be sure to phrase the question so that it yields the answer you need to know. For instance, if you are Jewish seeking another Jew, this question may find you a devout Christian, which may not suffice. Be specific in your asking.

- *Why* **did your last, or other, relationships end?**

  There will be so many clues in the answer to this question about how this person relates to intimacy, what they value and what their priorities are. They, too, have patterns and there is a good chance this person will behave the same way with you. It is so common for us women to want to believe that we will be the one who changes him or that he won't act this way with us, because his previous (or current) woman was (fill in the blank), and we are not (as though getting this person is a prize). I can tell you, there are times when he is no big prize. Instead, the big *surprise* is when you wake up and find yourself in the same or similar position, receiving the same complaints he made about the last one.

- *How* **did you end your last relationship?**

  This question is a spin on the previous one, because their M.O. now will likely be their M.O. again. Are they still friends? Did he leave taking care that they both worked out their issues so they could, at a minimum, be civil? Or is he angry and feeling slighted? Just notice. Pay attention. His attitude may tell you that he is not yet ready for a new relationship, as he is still healing from the last one. Or it may indicate his level of sophistication when it comes to dealing with his feelings. Again, simply notice what he does. Communicate responsibly, and trust your intuition. While not all past behavior is an indicator of things to come, most red flags are pretty obvious; for example, if he isn't paying child support, if he dumped his partner without trying to work things out, if he uses foul or derogatory language to describe his ex, and so on.

- **How do you get along with your family of origin?**
  This will tell you about his family values and his existing
  wounds, or lack thereof. Especially, how does he feel about
  his mother? If a man hates his mother, look out. Make
  sure that he has done work on himself and has found
  psychological resolve, because how he feels about women
  in general stems from his relationship with his mother!
  Does he respect her, feel smothered by her, ignore her,
  resent her, feel obligated to her, hold her in high regard,
  feel grateful for her years of loving support, admire her?
  Pay attention here! And don't forget to ask yourself the
  same questions about your relationship with your father. I
  have yet to meet someone who had a perfect childhood or
  a "normal" family, yet unresolved resentments can easily get
  projected onto a spouse or partner.

- **How do you feel about marriage?**
  If he's had a string of bad ones he will likely be
  uninterested. And NO, this is not an invitation to be the
  one who changes his mind! Even if he does change his
  mind, you will always feel like you manipulated him and
  he may feel manipulated, thus never giving himself to you
  wholeheartedly.

  I had a colleague and friend tell me that as soon as she
  knew she wanted to get married and have children, she
  decided to tell any man she was seriously interested in
  what her intentions were, right up front. She was seeing
  two men, both of whom she really liked. One told her that
  he was not interested in getting married for quite some
  time, but the other one said he wanted that for himself.

She took care to mention to them that she had not decided on any man yet, but that out of integrity she thought each of them should know. I loved hearing that and so appreciated her level of self-esteem, self-worth and respect.

- **Do you want to have children (or more children)? Do you already have children?**
  I have seen this topic rip people apart, especially now that folks are waiting longer to have children and then find it hard to get pregnant.

  If you are younger or older than your prospective mate, this will be an exceptionally important question—and ladies, LISTEN to the answer to this question. The last thing we need are more dads who are absent! If you have never had children, raising them by yourself is the hardest thing you may ever do. And unfortunately, our kids suffer even in the best-case scenario: where you love them and want them but are absent yourself because you are away all day trying to make a living and are stressed and unsupported! Your children absorb it all. For your sake and theirs, if you want children or don't want children, say it; take a stand and don't negotiate. You don't get a chance to undo this one! Due to its level of importance in people's lives, the answer to this one question can be a deal-breaker, so be sure to ask.

  Also, when a man tells you he does not want children with you, getting yourself pregnant will not likely change his mind on the matter. Tricking people usually backfires, and the child will be the biggest loser in the end. Do not use your body or your child as a way to get someone, or to find someone to take care of you. Take care of yourself; then find a partner you can stand beside. In the long run, you'll respect yourself for it and have a better shot at finding someone who wants the same things you do.

Funny, but many people neglect to mention that they already have children. One case that comes to mind is that of a man who had said no to having children, but didn't mention the fact that he was seeing someone who he had gotten pregnant. He didn't mention it because he had no intention of marrying the woman, and the child wasn't born yet. You just never know—unless you ask.

- **Have you ever been in jail?**
  You probably have not been in jail, but it doesn't hurt to know if he has been there; it could be a deal-breaker, depending on the infraction. Perhaps, as in my case (when I finally asked), the person you are seeing has been in jail several times, including for a DUI and attempted manslaughter. The person I interviewed had hit and seriously injured a little girl, and had spent six months in jail. Does this make him a bad person? Heavens, no. In this case, he was the sweetest, most loyal, adoring man in many ways. But it did tell me that he was a sick person who struggled with an addiction. Which, given my background, was a deal breaker.

And there are other legal and moral deal breakers, such as dealing drugs, addictive gambling, theft, violence, spousal abuse, being a sex offender; the list goes on. Refer to your non-negotiables. You will be surprised at what you can find out about someone if you genuinely care to know! By that same token, you may well be surprised what a quick Google search turns up. A little effort can reveal a lot.

- **Have you ever done hard drugs or sold drugs?**
  Heroine, crack, meth? Do they have track marks? A history of rehab? Lost a job because they drank too much or drank on the job? Do they use drugs recreationally, such as cocaine or ecstasy? Does that fit in with your lifestyle and values?

- **Do you have a sexually transmitted disease?**
  I have heard countless stories. As one might imagine, this subject is very delicate, and likely brings up shame and other related feelings, because people may have had an experience where someone left them as a result of telling the truth. On the other hand, herpes is so common now that there are pharmaceutical ads for treatments on television, like it's no big deal—but for some of you, it might be.

  Talking about STD is tricky. I've heard people say, "Well, she/he never asked." And also, some folks don't even know they have an STD. Especially if we are talking about HIV, which infects hundreds of thousands of women each year in this country. It's better to be safe than sorry. Use protection if you are going to get physically involved—even if you asked and he said he doesn't have an STD. Get a test, ask him to get tested, and practice safer sex until you know for sure! It's the responsible, self-loving thing to do!

- **What are your goals for the next five, ten years?**
  It's good to find out what people are committed to! This

question will help you see what you both have in common. So often, if we merge as a result of chemistry, we end up feeling resentful when our partners don't share the same interests we do—and I don't mean fake interests. Some of us pretend to like sports just to get the other person to be with us. Or we pretend we are interested in camping, when in fact we hate dirt and would rather poke our eye out than sleep outside. This all comes to a head when you have recently had a child and he wants to celebrate your first weekend away together at Camp Borcunga, while you would far rather go to the Ritz!

You also want to know if he has plans to go back to school, or travel around the world, or write a book, or give up his well-paying career to become a wildlife photographer in Africa. These are things you should know, and he should know about you too. Honestly, after the glow shifts and changes, as it does in all relationships, you want to have a good deal in common for a strong, healthy relationship. Unless, that is, you prefer not to see your partner often, and want to sleep in different rooms (or maybe different cities), because that's what is at stake if you don't take the time to explore this topic.

- **What are you passionate about?**
  This is a fun question to ask, and the answer can be equally telling! Listen up, there is a lot here. People can be passionate about politics, travel, their families, their work, finding a cure for cancer, athletics, literature, art, music, and so on. Find out how that shows up for the person you're interested in and if his passions are ones you want to share, support, and learn about—or want nothing to do with.

Because it's not likely to change, unless he is the kind who gets passionate about something new every few months or weeks—and this, too, is good to know, especially if you are considering a more stable, quiet arrangement.

I have seen a number of people get torn apart here as well, because they felt like a second fiddle, as though their partner's passion was a mistress that they had to fight for scraps of attention.

How to Ask!

Knowing what to ask, and then asking, are worlds apart for some people. Unfortunately, we cannot reap the benefits of simply thinking about asking the important and tough questions, just as we are not judged by our good intentions. Here action counts! Yes, there is a lot to know; and yes, it will probably take a good amount of time to find out. It's not likely you're going to sit down with a pad of paper and rattle off your list like a journalist, which is probably inappropriate in most cases, unless you are practicing, which I do recommend (sans the pad)!

You will need to slow down, and why not? At the end of the day, you have you, your passions, your commitments and your life (which is rich and full); a relationship is the cherry on the sundae of it all . . . right? If your answer is no, reread the previous chapters. Spend more of your time and energy loving yourself, connecting inside with The Great Divine, and you will get there!

Here are a few tips and reminders to get you started:

- **Love does not have a shelf life**, chemistry does! If you think some, or any, of these questions will scare your potential partner away, then you have your information right there. Love, as my husband reminds me, is a verb, not a noun! Anyone who is partner material will appreciate your inquiry and will understand that you are a discerning person who is taking care of herself by inquiring!

- **Asking tough questions with heart** is always a good place to start. While it's important to ask, *the way we ask* is also something to consider. Take care to be gentle and graceful when asking tough questions. While this should go without saying, it is worth mentioning because sometimes, when we get nervous, we can seem too direct or suspicious. Be interested in this person; show your curiosity with respect and compassion.

- **Take your time.** If this person is who you think or feel they are, let it unfold naturally, keeping in mind you probably don't want to drop your drawers (i.e., get physically intimate) before you know the answers to the most important things on your list.

- **Don't limit yourself to these questions,** rather let these be the beginning of some thought-provoking and soul-searching discussions based on other topics of importance specific to you. Use your non-negotiable list from chapter 6 to guide you in developing your own personalized list of questions.

If you need further support, our contact info is in the back of the book. You can email us, sign up for a telephone consultation, or check out my blog and let us know what you would like to learn more about. Also, check out the resource list in chapter 11 to meet my favorite wise teachers.

Chapter Eight

The Compass

As long as you think that the cause of your problem is out there—
as long as you think that anyone or anything is responsible for your
suffering—the situation is hopeless. It means that you are forever
in the role of victim, that you're suffering in paradise.
—BYRON KATIE

Heather was a well-educated, successful, never-been-married gal with a string of long-term relationships, and her baby alarm clock recently had started to tick. As she neared forty, she started contemplating her shelf life. The peculiar thing was that while she seemed to have her act together—an enviable career, a tight circle of close friends and family, and was healthy and fit—she had a knack for attracting Mr. Wrong (charming, generous and utterly emotionally obtuse) over and over and over again. For Heather, it appeared the only thing *they* all had in common, aside from knowing *her*, was that they all knew each other. It was at least a place to start.

"You have to listen to this message," Heather said as she eagerly rummaged through her voicemails to find the one she wanted me to hear. "Wait . . . here it is. Listen." She pushed her BlackBerry up to my ear.

"Waaaay are ya? . . . Heather . . . I'm comin' ta git ya," the man on the other end of the line slurred, barely audible. She pulled the phone away from my head and saved the message. *Curious,* I thought, *a clue.*

"Can you imagine a grown man like that? He left ten messages on my phone that night, he was so drunk!"

I didn't have to imagine; I had had my fair share of drunken encounters with men, thank you very much, and honestly didn't miss any one of them.

"You know," she continued, "over the weekend, my girlfriend and I were wondering, where are all the normal guys? Remember when you tried to set me up with that guy, Simon, the guy who had the fetish for wearing women's undies?"

"Come on, that's not fair, he seemed nice; and anyway, who knew? That's not something I would have thought to ask him! Besides, you figured him out before he got into yours, right?"

Heather laughed. "Those could have been my undies he was wearing." She did have a point.

It was always a bit precarious, picking the *good ones* for someone else. Pre-screening wasn't foolproof, even with a pro like me. We happened to find out from another gal who dated him that he had a serious fetish for wearing women's panties, which, in my book, would have been a deal breaker—but hey, to each her own.

The next time I saw Heather, she was back *on* with a fella that she had been seeing off and on for the last year or so. I had met him once or twice, and by appearances he was nothing like the last one. That one had been big and tall; this one was short and small. They didn't seem to have anything in common, aside from liking to ski, which was at the top of Heather's non-negotiable list: He must ski. I didn't know much else about her criteria. She kept her cards pretty close to her chest, but that was about to change. I decided I would make it my business to know.

"How's it going?" she asked in that plucky way she had. I had learned, over time, that she preferred the less direct approach. A fair amount of sincere chitchat usually did the trick; and once she warmed up, she was raring to go.

"So how's . . . ?" I asked casually.

"Ross," she said tentatively.

"Right, Ross."

"You know, things are good . . ." What was so interesting about Heather was her noticeable contradictions. Her demeanor was like that of a surfer, yet at first blush she looked like a blue blood. Her fresh face was never made up, her ears were dolloped with standard pearl earings, and she had product-free blonde hair with straight bangs. Yet, if you took a second look, you would notice her plummeting cashmere neckline, some fabulous piece of jewelry that made a strong architectural statement, and the tiniest pearl at the top of her left earlobe. Her style was a mix (more New York than California) of Andy Warhol meets Princess Diana.

"What did you guys do this weekend?"

"You know, at some point, you'd think people would just grow up!"

I didn't have a clue what she was talking about, but knew exactly what she meant.

"Ross and I were supposed to go out. It was my birthday last week; so he calls me two hours after we were supposed to meet, after I had been texting him for the last hour. And he didn't know why I was so upset." She was noticeably still upset. I winced a bit, hating that I had forgotten her birthday myself. "He was, like, 'You were with your girlfriends so what's the big deal? You knew my friends were in from Chicago this weekend and that I had had a really stressful day and—' Then he goes, 'You don't have my back, Heather.' So he keeps callin' me," She looked down at her phone, which was beeping like crazy. "But I'm going to ignore him."

She said that resolutely, but I could tell it was really bothering her. I had been through a few of these relationships with Heather, and she wasn't one to cry or even complain about men. She got busy instead.

"What happened?"

"He was out partying with his friends and, you know, lost track of time."

"So what had you agreed to do?"

She thought for a minute. "He was going to meet me for dinner, and I called and called him and he just blew me off."

"Heather, you didn't answer my question. Tell me what you had agreed to about your birthday. What did you hear him say?"

"It's not even that. He didn't even get me a *card* on my birthday. Nothing. Not breakfast in bed . . . not even . . . sex! I mean, come on, no sex on your birthday? What is wrong with that picture? And then he blows me off when we were going to have dinner to celebrate it, A WEEK LATER! And then . . . says *I* don't have *his* back."

I acknowledged her and then paused, making sure she was done with that thought. Then I asked another equally direct and potentially grating question. "Is this consistent with his behavior?" She looked at me, unclear. "I mean, is this his M.O.? Does he say one thing and do another . . . consistently?" I suspected, by the look on her face, that she was calculating the frequency. She got it.

"I know that when I expect people to be what they are really not, I get disappointed," I said. "If this is his deal and you are not okay with it, you need to tell him. But just for fun—okay, this might not be fun, but go with me here. What is he doing that you are having a hard time with? Is it that he forgot your birthday, or is it that he always chooses his friends over you? Or you think that he is too self-centered?"

"It's just that sometimes, when he starts partying, he loses track of time; and I am sick of it. It's not like I don't go out with my friends and have a good time, but it's always about him—that he's had a bad day or what he's going through—and . . . "

"Did it hurt your feelings that he didn't make a big deal out of your birthday?"

She laughed out loud in her husky way. "That he didn't make *any* deal out of it is more like it. And we aren't having sex. That's just wrong."

"So is it that you're not having enough sex?"

"Any."

"Is it that you're not having *any* sex, then?"

"I was at a party this weekend and was totally disgusted—all these people I have known for years were sitting around doing a crazy amount of drugs, and I thought . . . *Grow up!* It was ridiculous. I am over it."

I was doing my best to see what was really at the core here. "So does Ross do a lot of drugs, Heather?" I took a chance on another approach, being privileged to know her last two long-term relationships were with guys that partied pretty hard.

"He doesn't do it every day; it's just that when he does it . . . I don't know." She trailed off again.

"So is it that he does drugs too often that bothers you?" I asked, trying, to get back to the line of inquiry.

"I think it's that, and everything. I just want to take a break. I feel like he doesn't get it."

"Okay, so just to finish my thought about the little process."

She rolled her eyes.

"Come on, this is really great stuff! If you could pick one or two things he's 'doing to you' or that you can't stand, what would they be?"

"Hmmmm, I guess I would have to say that he's really unmotivated to do anything with me. It's always me suggesting things. Maybe that's it," she said.

"Are you sure that's it? In this process, I would let myself get really clear on what I think the other person is doing 'to me,' or I would name the behavior that I am reacting to. I'd really judge it fully, so I am crystal clear. Does that feel clear, that he's unmotivated to initiate activities with you, or is there something more specific?

"What do you mean?" she asked.

"I am just saying that it makes it easier to see the truth when you are clear here. What does it mean that he is unmotivated to initiate activities? What are you really saying about him? What is the judgment?"

"Uhmmm, that he doesn't initiate because he doesn't care to?"

"That feels closer to me. Does that seem more accurate?"

"Yes."

"So what would be even closer to what you perceive to be the truth?"

"That he doesn't care enough about *me* to make the effort," she admitted sadly.

"We can stay with this, because you have hit some feelings, which is a clue that we are closer to the truth here. Let's look at the next part of this process. The judgment is, he doesn't care enough about you to make the effort to . . . whatever." I said trying to recap. "Now, Heather, where do you not care about yourself? Where don't you make the extra effort with yourself?"

She just raised her eyebrows as if to say, *Good question.*

> *If I don't know what I feel, I don't know what I need.*
>
> ♏

I continued. "The thing about this process is it helps get things in perspective; because, like I always say, *If I don't know what I feel, I don't know what I need.* Most often we are so busy reacting to people's behavior and then, rather than looking inward, we blame them for not meeting our needs or not doing whatever's right. This inquiry allows us to slow down a bit and see what's really going on with us. Then we can take a look at being responsible for how we react or respond. That's the next and, honestly, more difficult part.

"In real time this definitely takes some practice, but right now you can see that you weren't really upset at what Ross was doing. You were upset about what you were making it mean. What it *may* have meant. But, we can't change people! I asked if this was consistent with his behavior, because if it is, you have a choice about communicating that to him. That is the other part of this process—responsible communication. It is your responsibility, especially in an intimate relationship, to let the person know what your expectations and needs are, rather than reacting every time he disappoints you. And now you have some language. You took care to see what the projection was, and by owning it, you gained some understanding (and hopefully, compassion) with which you ideally will be able to communicate to Ross."

I could see this was complex, and she was a bit lost. "Okay, so it's like this:

1) Ross did (fill in the blank)? (Be specific as you can.)

2) What did you make that mean? Take responsibility for it.

3) Find that behavior in yourself. (Identify what you are feeling. If you don't know what you feel, you don't know what you need.)

4) Own the projection!

5) Communicate your need to your partner—that this is important to you. And, like I always say, they will grow or go!

"So, number one, Ross was . . . ?" I started her off so she could really get what I deem the most liberating tool of all: taking responsibility for your reality and communicating responsibly.

"Ross was not acting like he cared about me; I mean, he wasn't going out of his way to show me he cared about me."

"Great, then two, what did you make that mean?"

"That he didn't care about me."

"Three . . ."

"And where do I not care about myself? Uhhh, yeah I see, sort of. And that makes me feel sad and unloved, I guess. And I should try and give that love to myself is where I get a little lost. This is hard," she said.

"Yes," I said with a smile, "hard, frustrating, confusing—but it beats the hell out of the alternative, which, babycakes, is having more of what you've got! So yes, love yourself more. Part of that will be communicating to Ross what you need." This was the place she locked up, where most of us do.

Communicating one's needs is the part that I notice separates the men from the boys—or in this case, the girls from the women. "It's the other part of practicing responsible communication: telling yourself the truth and then communicating that truth to your partner, as needed." I said.

"Okay, do I tell Ross I don't think he cares about me?"

"If that is really what you believe. But, if you see that Ross didn't do anything to you, take responsibility for your experience. He is mirroring your own lack of self-love. Maybe you will want to let him know what love looks like for you. For example, 'Ross, my birthday is a really big deal for me and it hurt my feelings that you didn't keep your commitment for dinner.' Then watch what he does with that. If he does care about you, he will listen intently, especially if you are not in reaction. And then he'll let you know if he can, or wants, to meet your expectation or need—which will tell you a lot about what he values.

"The relationships that are the most solid are the ones where both people are devoted to the truth, have generous hearts, and are happy to please from a genuine place. If this is really important to you, then your partner—*someone who wants what you want for yourself*—will be more than happy to make a big deal out of your birthday, while supporting you in deepening your commitment to your own practice of self-care and self-love."

> *The relationships that are the most solid are the ones where both people are devoted to the truth, have generous hearts, and are happy to please from a genuine place.*

I could see we were done. I told her the story about the lady walking down the street who fell into the hole. She loved it. Then we hugged, and she left.

> **GREAT ALLEGORY FOR GROWTH**
>
> A lady walking down the street falls into a hole. It takes her a while, as she is hurt and doesn't know how to get out; but ultimately she figures it out. The next day the same lady walks down the same street and forgets the hole is there. She falls in again. This time, however, she remembers how to get out and does so as quickly as she can. The next day, the same lady walks down the same street, sees the hole, falls in anyway, and—you guessed it—hops right out. The next day the same lady walks down the same street, sees the hole but walks around it. Eventually, the lady decides to walk down a different street!

HINDSIGHT:
THE COMMON DENOMINATOR IS ALWAYS YOU

I adored Heather and wanted so much for her to have what she wanted, what we all want: a healthy, loving, fulfilling relationship starting with ourselves! I knew that, just like me, she would find it when she was ready, when she had enough of what she didn't want, and then she would do whatever it took to get it. Shortly thereafter, she told Ross what she was feeling and what was important to her about her birthday, a definite breakthrough for her. I knew she was on her way.

Heather signed up for my seminar shortly after my mini-soapbox session. She saw how the exercise I taught her fit nicely with a practice of self-care, the importance of understanding and being clear on what she wanted, and the skill of interviewing her potential partners well. While each tool is not predicated on the last (each of us may find ourselves more adept in some areas than others), it's nice to reflect and see where we could use a tune-up or could develop a new skill that we didn't even know we were missing.

Heather saw how she had, like most of us, been attracted to the same type of guy for reasons that, prior to the seminar, had escaped her, and how trying to change him doesn't work—or isn't even the point. The point was about loving and changing what she could in herself, and communicating her desires and needs to whomever she chose to be intimate with.

The next time I saw Heather I asked how her relationship was going.

"I fell in the hole again!" she said, and laughed. I was delighted she was comfortable being that open, as well as more self-aware. I was confident Heather knew how to get out of that hole now and would when she was good and ready.

All relationships are breeding grounds for growth. As a result of her continuing to expand and develop her tool belt, Heather now had greater access to her own wisdom. She had learned the importance of self-inquiry, of being internally referenced, and of the power in taking responsibility for her choices and her life.

THE TOOL: THE COMPASS

The basic premise of the Compass is to take responsibility for your reality in the way you communicate. Often we hide behind our assumptions and expectations, lacking the courage to speak with real authority because we are manipulative and divisive. We try to get our needs met through coercion, rather than being open, honest and straightforward. Sometimes we spend so much time looking at, blaming and rationalizing others' poor conduct so that we don't have to look at our own issues of low self-esteem, lack of clarity and little self-respect. Unfortunately most of us play the blame game: we blame our feelings, disappointments and overall reality on our partners, and react or become unreasonably emotional when things don't go our way.

Many of us are heavily invested in being a victim, believing if "they" would (fill in the blank) everything would be okay. The truth is you ARE responsible for your reality—what you feel, what you need and how you communicate. The Compass will help you make sure you keep the arrow point at YOU, not "them." It took me years of believing the needle always pointed at them before I understood what a losing battle this belief was, and even longer before I really got it. The good news is, I am always the problem *and the solution!*

I noticed in my own life that no matter who I was in relationship with, blaming anyone for my feelings or experience was a dead-end street. As a matter of fact, it created the opposite of what I really wanted.

> *The good news is,*
> *I am always the problem*
> *and the solution!* ♏

I spent so many years of my life reacting to everyone and everything that I became trigger-happy: I stopped putting my authentic self out there and became overly vigilant at seeing how others were going to be, react and respond, and spent all my energy either preparing for that or dodging it.

When I woke up and realized that the common denominator in all my experiences, in all my relationships and in my life was *me*, everything started to change for the better. I began to take responsibility for my reality instead of staying stuck in the victim loop, believing things happened to me, rather than deciding for myself how it was going to be and navigating it. Responsibly communicating is the crux of this tool.

The most powerful freedom I know is to take responsibility for your reality *in its entirety* and then, rather than reacting, to respond accordingly. No one is doing anything to me: it is my job to communicate my needs responsibly! This is the natural progression when we understand and start to behave in accordance with being internally referenced.

Inquiring about the nature of

> *When I woke up and*
> *realized that the*
> *common denominator*
> *in all my experiences,*
> *in all my relationships*
> *and in my life was me,*
> *everything started to*
> *change for the better.* ♏

your feelings, your own or someone else's, can be very uncomfortable, so be kind and gentle. Just remember, if you forget which direction to look for your answer, the arrow on the Compass is pointing back at you too!

A useful tool I created for myself was to name what I blamed in my partner—for example, "You're selfish, uncaring, insensitive, not listening to me, not considering my needs!" and then notice whatever my initial reaction was. I really let myself have several minutes to get into it so I could get the truth of my projection. Then, I would take it on. Own it, find it in me. I really took care and had the courage to see where I possessed that same trait or behavior somewhere in my own life, which magically gave me compassion—or, at minimum, understanding. Then I could take responsibility for what I had experienced.

> *Taking responsibility for your reality is liberating and in alignment with the highest truth.*
> 𝒳

The next level of maturity and sophistication was to see how I actually created the situation myself. Because, as we have learned, how you are with yourself, what you believe about yourself, and how you treat yourself—these are how you see and perceive the way you are with others. This was, for me, one of the most liberating tools of all. To be free from the blame game—I had never realized that could happen! The equally important point of this tool is to communicate your wants and needs responsibly, instead of assuming someone should know, be a mind reader or guess at what your needs are and then blaming them when they don't get it right! In the following chapters we will look more closely at how to express your needs and make agreements.

> *Speaking what you want gives you the greatest likelihood of having what you want.*
> 𝒳

EXERCISE: CELEBRATE YOURSELF

Love does not alter the beloved; it alters itself.
—SOREN KIERKEGAARD

So here you are—buffed and fluffed, internally referenced, and facing life from the inside out. You have taken a good look at yourself—where you spend your energy, what your self-sabotaging patterns are—and given quite a bit of thought to what you want (and what you don't want). You have taken steps, some of them deep and intense, cementing an internal foundation of self-love and care. You have a practice of self-

> *The answer to everything is always within you!* 𝓜

inquiry; a direct line to The Divine, 24/7; a Self-Love Rx; and a list of non-negotiable issues to help keep you on your path. You know what questions to ask your potential partners, and you know how to ask them. And you have a tool belt fit for a Relationship Queen as you venture out into your new life, which will be a perfect reflection of all the work and care you have invested into yourself.

Now what? I'll tell you—*it's time to celebrate!* It is time to celebrate yourself, and I mean that in the most literal sense.

Right about the time I found myself in this very place—having spent many years learning to love myself, falling in and out of "manholes" along the way, practicing my tools, taking myself for long walks, listening to my own feelings, adding to my wish list and my non–negotiable list, practicing my interviewing skills, sitting with myself in self-inquiry, practicing turning all these tools into skills, evolving characteristics I wanted in a partner and in myself—I noticed something very surprising. It dawned on me that if I wanted to be in a committed relationship, I had to choose me first. I needed to literally make a commitment to myself before I could make a commitment to anyone else!

I saw that setting boundaries with others and keeping my self-love practice going was absolutely important, but that if I ever wanted a real commitment, I needed to make a sacred commitment to myself first. Then, out of nowhere, I had a brilliant idea—to marry myself! That's right, marry me! I suddenly knew this was what I needed if I wanted someone true and committed to himself, true and committed to me, and to be all the things I was working on being. It suddenly was obvious.

Coincidentally, I had developed (post my own divorce, of course) a little pet peeve about people who got married and took their vows lightly; or tossed them altogether whenever they felt like things didn't go their way; or bailed because they couldn't handle the truth when they discovered who they really were—warts, wounds and all. So I thought I would put my money where my rather large mouth was and do it, actually marry myself. Even though I did not propose, per se (that seemed a little *too* weird for me), I did see that taking care to create a commitment ceremony for myself would perhaps prepare me at last for a grown-up, healthy, fulfilling, sustainable, committed relationship with someone else!

So I did it—and I mean I really did it. I proceeded as though it were a traditional marriage. I picked a venue, somewhere incredibly sacred to me. I bought a dress, a long fancy gown. I included my son, invited my closest friends (you should have seen the look on the ladies' faces when I told them I was marrying myself) and wrote vows to myself that later I would turn into something I call a Consciousness Agreement. I even had a ring made that to this day I love and wear proudly: It has seven gems that represent what I am most committed to. And I even had a reception afterwards! It was a momentous occasion and one that transformed my relationship with life, what it meant to be committed and how much I meant to myself. Words cannot adequately explain how this changed me as a person; it was as though it rearranged my DNA.

Here are the vows I read aloud:

- I promise to continue to seek the truth in my heart, body, mind and spirit.

- I promise to stay committed to my path of consciousness and agree to do all that is in my power to stay awake so that I may better do God's will.

- I promise to be true to myself and to be all that I teach and share with you.

- I will do my very best to refrain from judgment.

- I vow to clean up any situation where I may have caused harm.

- I will do my best to stay when I want to run and to open when I want to shut down to protect myself, knowing that in my vulnerability I will eventually find true strength.

- I vow not to have to always be right or to always have to know everything.

- I will allow myself to stand alongside you and be fully human, with all my flaws and ugliness, beauty and radiance, so that I may share this journey fully with you.

- I vow to be your Mirror as you are my own, to let myself fall off my path without ridicule or judgment, and to do my best to get back on.

- I vow to let you fall off your path, as well, with the same grace and dignity, and to invite you back to the celebration of your life, as seamlessly as possible.

- I vow to remind you, as you remind me, that in every moment there is an opportunity to reunite with God and to stay awake in consciousness.

- I vow to aspire to a life filled with gratitude, abundance for all, and peace on earth. I pray that we all find peace in ourselves so that we practice goodwill toward each other.

The funniest thing happened several weeks later. I was sitting at my desk, the glow having worn off as I came out of the "honeymoon" phase. I was running some old negative story about myself, having fallen back asleep temporarily—when all at once, sick of hearing the bloody story repeat again, I declared: "I want a divorce!" and then began to laugh hysterically at the absurdity of it.

In any event, I can tell you that this ceremony was one of the most important decisions and self-loving actions I have ever made and taken. Having come from parents who divorced, I watched the divorce rate soar and had a failed marriage myself. I had become pessimistic about what it meant to actually be committed and if it were even possible. That is, until I found the answer: A committed relationship is only possible to the degree it is possible with myself.

Happily Ever After Exists After We Commit to Love Ourselves

I felt incredibly fortunate, feeling in love with life, my son, my work, my purpose; and I wasn't greedy. Maybe not everyone gets the soul mate; I was okay with not getting one. Yet in attendance the day that I married myself was a man who at the time had become a dear and true friend, someone who resonated deeply with my vows and my commitment to my path. He was someone who—after I put him through the ringer, interviewing him like a special op-agent, setting boundary after boundary, spending endless days and precious hours of processing and inquiry—eventually became the loving, devoted, adoring husband that I am blessed to share my life with today!

Wow, I still pinch myself (and have a long list of friends who want to know if he has a brother). I am grateful I have had the courage to follow my inner guidance, and am forever grateful to know there are men, like my husband, who are healthy, loving and emotionally available. Which reminds me of a quote I displayed prominently at our engagement party: "THAT WHICH YOU SEEK IS SEEKING YOU!"

Perhaps you are thinking that a formal marriage to yourself is a little over the top. I invite you, at least, to create a sacred ceremony of some kind. For example, you can write your vows to yourself and make saying them a part of your Daily Practice, or do whatever you feel is appropriate. You might want to share your vows with another person—perhaps someone you currently seek spiritual guidance from, or maybe a special friend that you trust. Say your vows aloud. There is something so powerful about declaring what you are committed to and what you stand for. This also allows your nearest and dearest to help hold you accountable! Maybe you want to gather a few close friends who you feel would support you, who would see the value in your decision, and hold the vision, to listen as you make this commitment aloud.

> *THAT WHICH YOU SEEK IS SEEKING YOU!*
> ℳ

At the end of my seminar, we spend an entire day celebrating each participant's commitment to herself. Each gal dresses up to suit herself, reads her vows aloud, invites friends or family to attend and places something precious on an altar that we create together to always remind her of this day. It is incredibly beautiful—and however hokey, scary or over-the-top participants may have thought the idea was at first, there is never a dry eye in the place by the end of the ceremony. Each woman's expression touches the rest. Some dance, sing, read poetry, or just stand in silence as the rest of us bear witness to her special day. Maybe that's the way for you, too. Get a group of other women who want to make the same commitment to themselves, and go for it! We have all thrown parties for lesser reasons.

It is important here to remind you that having a Daily Practice will help you stay on your path of being committed to yourself and that it is how to stay focused on your future vision. Staying connected to your inner guidance really is what bridges that gap between you and what you long for—deep peace, inner satisfaction and happiness. Don't forget to have a honeymoon too! You deserve it.

Chapter Nine

The Hammer

Assumptions are the termites of relationships.
—HENRY WINKLER

My husband and I were out to dinner and ran into a student of mine, Sylvia. After she and I excitedly embraced, she enthusiastically presented her new beau, Alex. Turns out she had gotten involved with him physically, but had failed to have "the talk."

We invited them to sit down and somehow got on the subject of having children. In fewer than thirty seconds Alex blurted out, "Yeah, well, if she gets pregnant, I'm not going to support her being a stay-at-home mom. There's no way I can afford her designer boots habit. *No way!*"

Of course, I looked at her and said, "Wow, did you know that?"

Sylvia looked at me and said, as though she had not heard him, "Did I know what?" As many single moms can attest, in hindsight this would be called a *red flag*!

"Did you hear your man say he is unwilling to support you staying home or to financially support you if you get pregnant?"

"Uhh, I would, just, ya know, get a nanny. Anyway I'm not having a baby right now ... so ... ." She blew it off.

My husband and I looked at each other, knowing full well the next conversation they would be having would be about what to do if she got pregnant.

She also knew better; and yet, like most of us, she figured it was irrelevant to bring up since she wasn't trying to get pregnant! Uh uh uh!

I did get a phone call the next day, confirming my suspicions. She and her man had "the talk" right after we parted ways. They would be the better for it later, however uncomfortable it was at the time. It goes to show, you never know until you smarten up and ask! Then make sure it's part of a Consciousness Agreement—unless you don't mind raising a baby by yourself, among other things!

Hindsight: If You Don't Ask for It, You're Probably Not Going to Get It

What we can see from this story is a summary of how all the tools are applied. We need to love ourselves, be committed to ourselves, know what we want and what we don't, interview well, and communicate our needs responsibly. Then, we need to agree to live what I would call a more conscious life. I define consciousness as *being internally referenced and knowing the difference between your false self and your authentic self.* As a result, your outside matches your insides. The reality, though, is that most of ours do not.

In Alex's defense, he was being pretty clear about his intentions. He just wasn't doing it in a respectful way that reflected a conscious agreement between the two of them. This was more of a dictatorship—my way or the highway. Sylvia, for whatever reason, was not asking the pertinent questions, and was choosing not to pay attention to the answers given even before she asked. Mind you, this was a student of mine already well versed in the tools and well aware of what she needed to know before she dropped her drawers. She let the chemistry of love and lust lull her back to sleep, temporarily. You will need to be careful not to let this happen to you too.

Most of us come to relationship a little (or a lot) beat up. We have survived our childhood, and our plight of being a woman in a man's world;

and we often are still inclined to accommodate others' needs ahead of our own. Despite what we may have learned (what it takes to be conscious and how to have a healthy relationship), we often abandon this knowing in our haste to be united, to fall in love, because it feels better—or so we think. Unfortunately, which is largely why I wrote this book, the chemistry wears off and we are back to where we started: brokenhearted, angry, resentful, sad and alone. Or, in Sylvia's case, a potential single mom fighting for child support from a guy who judges how she spends money.

Maybe it's because we are too afraid to stand for what we want and need . . . and risk standing alone if we don't get it! As my own story painfully illustrated in chapter 1, our pursuit of our unconscious needs is usually largely based on our insecurity and wounds, and we continue to be in denial as we seek Happily Ever After. We don't ask, Happily Ever After what? I don't remember Cinderella saying, "Just because this glass slipper fits, doesn't mean I'm going to wear it. You and I need to have a little talk first, O Royal Prince—what is your name?" We overlook seeing if we have anything in common when we don't take care in the beginning to stand up for our non-negotiable issues and to set forth our parameters for being together. After the deadly combination of chemistry and dreams mixed with no real plan for the future, what we often get is a long-standing war of manipulation, compromise and in some cases violence, destroying any love we may have shared.

> *Get clear on what's important to you in a relationship.* ♡ᴍ

I simply wasn't willing to stay in an unhealthy relationship anymore, and I'm hoping you aren't either. I define unhealthy as indifference to my needs, a focus on my partner's needs almost exclusively, any kind of regular hostility or abuse, emotional neglect, and absence of trust and respect. What I *was* willing to do was to approach someone I had invested love, energy and time in a relationship with, to see if we had exhausted our resources. I needed to find out if there was any chance of fanning the flames and creating a healthy situation out of an unconscious one. Whatever the case is for you, the choice is yours—to now do something different. To take what you have learned and put it to the acid test.

THE TOOL: THE HAMMER

The Hammer — creating Consciousness Agreements — is one of the most powerful tools we can use to ensure that we get as close as we can to creating the most ideal environment in which people and relationships can thrive. No matter *who* you choose, you need to know where you stand and what you value and have an agreement with your partner about *how* you are going to be in relationship.

After all, now that you're *married* (to yourself), you get to have sex . . . right? Wait a minute. Let's slow down. I know, sex is natural, beautiful and meaningful; at least it can be. But it can also rip your tender heart out. That is, of course, unless you're among the less than one percent of people who meet someone, have sex right away and live Happily Ever After. (Please do send me stories of people happily, blissfully married for fifty or more years who started this way; so far, I have collected . . . let's see . . . uhhh, none.)

We get physical way too fast in our haste to be connected, and we all know what happens when we don't take care to negotiate our needs. I am not advocating, one way or the other, having sex before or after marriage. I am saying it is more difficult to avoid heartbreak and to undo bad habits and relationship patterns after we have had sex with someone. By then, the chemistry has taken effect. We say yes when we mean no (or should say no) and almost always compromise ourselves, because this intoxicating feeling and attachment renders us senseless.

For most of us, if we have sex with someone we are honestly interested in being in a real relationship with before we have let *them* know where we stand, it is almost ALWAYS a recipe for disaster. While

Samantha in the television show *Sex in the City* makes having casual sex seem attractive, in real life most women are not physically, emotionally or psychologically wired for such vapid intimate encounters. And if you don't believe me, let me know how *casual* you felt about it the last time you *made love* with someone you truly wanted to be with—and then they dumped you. Even the toughest of us are not immune to the heart's vulnerability in the unrequited-love story. But even if you have already done the deed, it is not too late to say what you want and need—it just makes it more complicated!

> *Identify your non-negotiables.* ♡

Before you get intimately involved, your non-negotiable needs— such as having children; fidelity; being an at-home mom or a career woman or a single mom—need to be said up front. Instead of selling your sex appeal for security, or your caretaking ability for validation (the sure way to meet disaster or, at minimum, resentment), why not be courageous and put what you want in writing by creating a Consciousness Agreement?

The leap from *me* to *we* is giant and should be considered carefully. So let's say you have done some of your homework, been busy turning these tools into skills and now face

> *Review your situation and each of the six tools.* ♡

the important decision of sharing your sacred self with another. These tools may be useful to you in phases. Perhaps, having first interviewed well, you have a good sense of what is to come. And now you want to be even more intimate. Right here is where most of us, like Sylvia, get into the deepest trouble. We start taking shortcuts, and as I say about myself, even come down with selective color-blindness: we temporarily lose our ability to see red flags.

The Hammer, along with the rest of the tools in your tool belt, can be really helpful for keeping your wits about you. This is the time to slow down. Make sure you are in agreement about what this next step means to both of you and how you intend to treat each other and your relationship. At minimum, be sure that you both are willing to take responsibility for the immediate realities that sex involves—disease control, birth control and potential parenting, as well as the emotional realities of becoming intimately involved.

> *Sex is the easy part of a relationship.*
> ♏

With all due respect, sex is usually the easy part of a relationship, so what the heck is the hurry? If he's all that, it is worth the wait; and if he *is* ALL THAT, he *will* wait! Sex is fun, yes. It feels good, yes. And honestly, it is worth it to wait. Because it clearly is not fun, nor does it feel good at all, to wake up with (or break up with) someone you didn't take the time to know and make agreements with first. Making sure you have a healthy foundation for a relationship is the *only* way you can ensure a higher likelihood of creating a healthy, fulfilling, sustainable relationship. Am I saying *all* relationships fail when people have sex right away? No, but most of those end, and badly at that.

If you love yourself and are in right relationship with yourself and life, you know there is no rush. That sense of urgency to merge physically is an old pattern and, frankly, most often it is a sign of desperation and emptiness. Yes, hormones are *powerful*. Yes, they make you feel like you can't help yourself; but the truth is, you always have a choice. Love has no shelf life. More often than not, if we hurry and have sex before we have taken care to see where we both are with each other and what we both want, we'll find ourselves smack in the middle of a similar, if not the same, story we were in last time. Are you willing to risk that? Again? Think about it!

And, anyway, now that you are internally referenced, you can see that there is less urgency to get sexually involved too soon. I could write a book on this one point, but for now, don't take my word for it, just look at your life. Look at your past relationships (go back to chapter 5 to review your patterns), and see for yourself how well it has worked when you've tried to negotiate your needs after the fact!

Imagine how different things would have been if you had taken the time to make agreements before you were intimately involved. The point of a Consciousness Agreement is not to change the other person or establish a set of rules that they must live by. Instead, it is a well-thought-out context for a healthy, fulfilling relationship, an agreement that includes your most important values, non-negotiables, and a spelled-out arrangement under which *both* you and your partner thrive together. What we are really talking about here is responsibility and creating a container within which each person is accountable to the other simply by being clear on their hopes, expectations and intentions.

Now I'll show you how to draft a Consciousness Agreement, *and* I'll even show you the first one that I wrote. This agreement is like having a personal creed, a declaration of inner-dependence. The next time some gorgeous man is in front of you, feel the comforting weight of the Relationship Tool Belt on your hip, pull out whichever tool is appropriate—Mirror, Magnet, Stud Finder, Flashlight, Compass, or Hammer—and invite him to build something with you! Look forward to crafting an amazing Consciousness Agreement together. If you have done all your homework, you'll nail this one easily.

EXERCISE: CRAFT YOUR CONSCIOUSNESS AGREEMENT

The most valuable thing I have learned about being
in a relationship is that you're not the only one in it.
—DREW BARRYMORE

You're ready to make the GIGANTIC leap from from ME to WE. At the precipice of a relationship, creating a Consciousness Agreement is so worthwhile because it sets the best possible climate for a healthy, fulfilling, sustainable relationship; yet it is precisely where most of us choke on our historic and genetic imprinting.

You might be asking, if we are taking care to love ourselves, if we know what we want, have impeccable interviewing skills and so on, why would we need to have an agreement? And what guy is going to go for that? Well, my dears, guyz probably wouldn't, but a man who wants the same things you do absolutely

> *People grow or they go.*
> ~

will! The psychological and physical act of creating a Consciousness Agreement helps you get crystal clear on where you stand *before you drop your drawers.*

Making the Leap from "Me" to "We"

Now perhaps you are not at the precipice of *new* love; rather, you have been on a journey of self-discovery while knee-deep in an ongoing relationship. You may be starting to intensify your path of growth midstream a relationship. You wake up inside a relationship and think: *What is going on here? Who is this person I am with and what have I done? OMG, I need to renegotiate here! I have to make it plain that I need (fill in the blank).*

Then you start to realize how you have compromised yourself. You look at this tool and think:

Too late for renegotiation; I have already sold my soul down the river. I am with someone who is set in his ways and will never go for what I really want. And how can I ask him to change the rules of the game midstream? Isn't that unfair? I told him I was into an open relationship, that it was okay to wait before we had kids, that I didn't mind that he traveled all the time, that I liked to watch sports, that I loved having sex three times a day, that pornography turned me on, that having separate bank accounts was fine. I said I didn't mind being his secretary even though I run two businesses of my own, that I loved to cook, that I didn't mind the way his kids treated me or that he was fat.

This would be a good time to review the vows you made with yourself. The first step in getting someone else to make and keep agreements with you is to be sure you are keeping the agreements you made with yourself.

Okay, so let's say you are currently in a relationship and the person you are with has made the final cut. You have interviewed or reinterviewed him; you are solid with your new path of self-love and self-commitment; you are practicing responsible communication, and now you are ready to say what you need, and you want to renegotiate. Go for it! I did. In my case, I had my own awakening, made the dramatic shift from being externally referenced to being internally referenced, and realized love did not happen outside myself.

From there, I was okay with whatever happened. I approached my partner to see if we could renegotiate our relationship in such a way that it was based on my true values and needs. Regardless of how he might respond, I now knew I had *me*, so I could not lose! That particular man was unwilling to look at himself and make any change at all. He stated clearly, "This is the way I am, take it or leave it." So, within a matter of months, I left him.

As I have said before, *people grow or they go.* However, this opening paved the way for me to meet the right man, one who was willing to honor my needs, and I, his. More importantly, he valued that I honored myself.

Now, you may find that your partner accepts the challenge to change the course of your relationship midflight. Fabulous! It's rarely too late, if you have picked a good partner, to renegotiate your agreement. By "good," I mean someone who has a Tool Belt, a set of relationship skills and a basic understanding of what it takes to be in a healthy relationship.

Your agreement may have been something you both needed to say out loud. Why not? People sign prenuptials in midstream of a relation-ship. This is even better! And then there are those of you who, like me, will end long relationships because it is plain that the person you are with refuses (or is too frightened or simply chooses not) to grow beyond where he is. Either way, you have yourself; and that, bottom line, is what will matter most. Indeed, the foundation for all things in your life is your relationship with yourself and with The Divine.

A Consciousness Agreement will help you establish, upgrade or make changes to support your relationship in becoming healthier, more fulfilling and ultimately sustainable.

You love each other, but somehow you're just not on the same page when it comes to money, birth control, kids, owning a home, career, partying, lifestyle choices or communication. First, I recommend that you back up and reestablish your foundation. Maybe you need to revisit some of the other tools first; writing a Consciousness Agreement may be putting the cart before the horse. Revisit the critical questions in chapter 7, as a means of knowing yourself and the other person better.

Make sure you are giving *yourself* what you need and not expecting your partner to be the sole provider of what you want. Check to see if you are communicating responsibly. If not, go back to the exercise on responsible communication on page 141. It will help you develop the skill of taking responsibility for your experience and reality.

Bottom line: this is an inside job. Observing your own behavior and working on yourself, rather than focusing on the other, is where your energy will be best spent. Stay focused on your commitment to yourself, and keep that in mind. Then come back to the relationship and see where you have not clearly spelled out what your agreements are.

You've got nothing to lose and everything to gain by making your desires clear and setting your agreements in writing. Trust me when I tell you that every man I have ever spoken to about this agreement loves it—that is, if he is sincere about being in a relationship that works. Men love success, and this is an excellent way of helping you both achieve that in your relationship!

Verbal Versus Written Agreements

When I created the Consciousness Agreement, I had just started spending time with the man who has become my husband, and I was ending a lifelong pattern of codependence and other unhealthy relationship issues. I was so committed to getting it right that I was overly vigilant, erring on the side of protecting my heart and soul. Having never met such a man, I was not sure he was for real. Even so, most of my initial Consciousness Agreements with him were verbal. I learned early on that he was a man of integrity, evidenced in every area of his life. His word was gold, and he honored all his agreements with others and with me; so I did not feel it necessary to write out how we would practice birth control or how we would go about resolving conflicts, or other basic things. We spoke them aloud, and he kept true to them, and still does to this day. He consistently did what he said, and I felt confident in these tacit agreements.

We did move into some more delicate and tender places as our relationship progressed, and I felt less sure that spoken words were enough. Still, my first written agreement was a declaration of what I was committed to; definitely a softer version than the verbal hell, endless inquisition, paranoia and tiny hoops my poor husband had to jump through before we ever even kissed!

After all that, I calmed down a bit, and he stayed long enough for me to see he was for real. Here is the first agreement I ever wrote:

Consciousness Agreement

- I ask that you hold me in my highest light, wishing only that I become the best version of what God would have me be as a whole, loving, human being; I will do the same for you.

- I ask that you honor my sacred boundaries with courtesy and care, as I will honor yours.

- I ask that you be responsible in your communication, as

well as that you own that your experience and your reality stem directly from inside of you.

- I ask that you communicate your feelings and thoughts with care, from the heart and with the sole intention of creating love and peace.

- I ask that we agree to self-inquiry first, seeking answers to all of our issues within ourselves.

- I ask that you hold my best interest in your heart at all times, and under all circumstances.

- I ask that we agree to responsible and respectful communication, refraining from harsh judgment and remembering the precious words, "There but for the grace of God go I."

And for you:

- I will do my very best to refrain from judgment.

- I agree to clean up any situation where I may have caused harm.

- I agree to try and stay, even when I want to run, and to open when I want to shut down to protect myself— knowing that in my vulnerability I will eventually find true strength.

- I agree not to have to always be right, or to always have to know everything.

- I will allow myself to stand alongside you and be fully human, with all my flaws, ugliness, beauty and radiance, so that I may share this journey fully with you.

- I agree to be your Mirror as you are my own, and to let myself fall off my path without ridicule or judgment.

- I agree to allow you the dignity of falling off your path, as well, and to invite you back to the celebration of your life, as seamlessly as possible.

- I agree to remind you, as you remind me, that in every moment there is an opportunity to reunite with God and to stay awake in consciousness.

- I agree to aspire to a life filled with gratitude, abundance for all, and peace on earth. I pray that we all find that peace in ourselves so that we practice goodwill toward each other.

- I agree our definition of love is, "I want what you want for yourself."

- I agree to laugh at myself regularly, and to laugh aloud as often as I can.

- It is my mission to help end human suffering and to do all that is in my power to help people help themselves. It is my vision to change the way our culture values women and shapes young people.

- May God bless you always and keep you safe from harm.

I'm sure you can see what a long way this Consciousness Agreement was from the rules I would have set forth way back in chapter 1. Your own agreement may focus on esoteric and spiritual topics, or physical daily responsibilities or a mixture of both. Explore until it feels exactly right for you.

Keep in mind that you don't have to have a partner to do this; you can create your Consciousness Agreement as a kind of affirmation or verbal vision of what you want. Remember, energy flows where attention goes, so your agreement alone can set the law of attraction into motion.

Crafting Your Agreement

You have already written vows to yourself, so this part is like writing vows for your relationship. Creating a Consciousness Agreement is about articulating to your partner what you want and need. So, play with it; start by writing a short agreement, and feel free to add to it. But do it!

While I know this is a big step—sometimes a giant leap from your practice of self-love and self-inquiry—most of you are either midstride a relationship already or are eager to get involved. You will not regret having taken care to spell it all out. Everyone wins, and that's how it ought to be.

Go ahead and grab those vows, your non-negotiables and some paper, or sit at your computer, and think about what you want to make sure is agreed upon before you get more serious. Begin crafting your Consciousness Agreement.

Here are some common examples of things you may want to include:

- We will wait for (fill in the blank) amount of time before we have sex.

- Here is what we will do if we get pregnant: (list)

- We will agree to practice birth control a certain way or for a certain period of time.

- We will agree to talk about issues when they come up, instead of waiting until they are huge.

- We will take responsibility for our experience in the relationship and avoid blaming each other.

- We will agree to seek counsel after a period of (fill in the blank) should we be unable to resolve a strong difference that is so important to one or both of us, that it may end the relationship if we don't resolve it amicably.

- We will agree not to actively pursue having children, because it isn't an option for one of us or negotiable at this time of our lives.

- We will agree to be financially independent in the areas of (fill in the blank).

- We will agree to be sexually exclusive, even though we are not married, for (fill in the blank).

- We will agree to live (fill in what area) until (fill in length of time). Example: "For the next three years, while I finish school, we will live near campus; then we can move to your preferred location."

- We will agree, should we decide to end this relationship for any reason, to seek counsel for at least six months first and to stay out of any other relationships until we are both clear that ours is over.

- We will agree to share the following responsibilities: (fill in the blank).

These are some practical examples. There are countless others I did not mention but that will probably come to mind as you work on your agreement (go ahead and write them down; don't be afraid!).

I hope that you take care, wherever you find yourself along your path in a relationship—at the precipice, knee deep, or up to your neck with another—to say what you mean and mean what you say. Let your word be your testament of integrity and impeccability. May you always stand up for yourself and say what you want or need, lovingly and responsibly!

Chapter Ten

Make Every Breath Count

Love is a promise, love is a souvenir,
once given never forgotten, never let it disappear.
—JOHN LENNON

You may have picked up this book at a point in your life where you were trying to find, get, or keep a man; yet by now, you will probably have figured out that the more "work" you do on yourself and with yourself, the more you inquire into and love yourself, the less what's going on out there really matters! Here's a love story about a woman, tool belt intact, who fell in love without a man.

I spent three years of my life watching, witnessing and participating in my girlfriend Naomi's battle with breast cancer. She was a person of great character, utterly devoted to practicing what she preached: living a life of impeccability, nonviolent communication and LOVE. She didn't just talk about being spiritual or having a practice; she lived it, even through her sob stories about men and relationships. Naomi had become a central part of my life, part of my family and my heart.

I watched her take the first blow of bad health news like a champ; it didn't knock her down for a moment. She took the first rounds of chemo, and even the following rounds of radiation, in fine form. Several months and three implant surgeries later, she came out swinging as we awaited the clean bill of health. Instead, we found out the cancer had grown, and migrated to her bones.

She hardly flinched, sitting on her yoga mat, continuing to teach and share her inspiration with us all. The Stanford graduate would prevail. She kept an online "boob log," danced, hiked, and lived life to the fullest in between more chemo, radiation and a growing number of drugs. Her lungs filled with fluid and her upper spine disintegrated from the radiation. More surgery replaced several inches of her spine with a steel rod; not good news at all for one who spent her livelihood as a yoga teacher. But Naomi saw the experience as an opportunity to practice her teaching, and she set a goal of being able to do a backbend within a year.

More chemo and more drugs followed, this time a harsh experimental concoction no one had ever seen. But that didn't deter this warrior goddess. Bald, sick, weak and now in a wheelchair, this woman, this amazing creature of will and courage, sat by my side to hear the news that the cancer had now traveled to her brain.

"What does this mean?" I wanted to know. "How long do we have? Will she ever be the same again? How will this affect her?"

The doctors recommended brain radiation. She asked, "Do we have a choice?"

"Not if you want to live any longer."

"Sign me up. Let's go!"

I remember our ferry ride over to San Francisco; we decided it was the most beautiful way we could travel on that clear summer's day. We met four construction workers on deck, and one of the younger guys asked Naomi and me what we were up to and if he could buy us a beer.

Naomi said, "I am dying, and I am going to get my brain radiated today," and then she smiled. Her attitude was a perfect outward reflection of her ongoing commitment to her practice of self-love and an ever-deepening connection to The Divine, despite her bleak prognosis.

The guy's mouth fell open. He started to smile, as though he thought she was pulling his leg. Then one of his buddies said, "Dude, I think she's serious."

We all fell silent as the boat pulled away from the five-knots-per-hour zone and out into the bay. She spent the rest of the boat ride listening to each of the guys tell a story of how he had lost someone close to him. She hung on their every word, giving them her full and undivided attention. Then the boat came to the dock, and with big hugs and blessings, we went on our way. She always found something to smile about.

You know that saying about how some people can take lemons and make lemonade? Naomi could have taken gasoline and made a birthday cake—an edible one!

After this last round of treatment she had a spike in energy, which we all hoped and prayed meant that maybe, just maybe, we would be blessed with a miracle: spontaneous remission. But we had to wait six weeks. Six long weeks of waiting and hoping and trying to be in the moment with her, because that's the only place she lived now—teaching us all the real meaning of presence and being here now.

Her optimism was contagious: she convinced the few hundred of us she called her "chosen family" that all was well. Then, as quickly as her spirits had lifted, they faded. Each day she showed more and more signs of slowing down and becoming weak, despite her metaphysical mindset. Her lungs began to fill with fluid again, and she could no longer travel even across the room without her oxygen tank. She couldn't sleep in any position other than the yoga child's pose, for no more than twenty minutes at a time. I took her to the hospital, where we went to the proverbial head of the line, and insisted that she get her scans *now*.

I wheeled her across the street and paced back and forth in the waiting room while I waited for them to see what was now so obviously terribly wrong. My warrior was starting to fade. After a while I sat down, because I knew other people there didn't need to pick up on my anxiety; they had their own stories to tend. And that's when I heard the whisper. The ethereal voice that I knew was God, The Great Spirit, The Divine. I heard, *It's time.* And after three years of praying, hoping and wishing, I knew, at last, it was her time to go.

The next day her doctor called to tell me Naomi had *maybe* six weeks left. That was heart-wrenching enough, but oddly nowhere near as mind-blowing as what Naomi shared with me that day.

In addition to being a woman who had achieved great discernment, spending most of her time in meditation or at her yoga practice, Naomi had become counsel to many, many friends and students over the years. On any given day, at least one—if not several—of them felt comfortable calling her and sharing some of their struggles and sorrows. On this day she shared one of them with me.

"That was my friend, Sasha," she said, with her now exceedingly gravelly voice. It sounded more like laryngitis than what it was; a tumor pressing relentlessly against her vocal cord. She put her cell phone away. "She's sad," she said, making an exaggerated sad face herself, her breath laboring at the end of every other word. "She's in so . . . much . . . pain, poor thing." She took another hit off her oxygen tank. I sat still and listened, waiting for her to gain her strength. She adjusted the tube that rested underneath her nostrils, and continued. "Her husband left her again . . . He . . . said . . . he didn't want to . . . do the married thing any . . . more." And then she paused and looked out the window.

I wondered what *didn't want to do the married thing anymore* meant. I didn't ask. I didn't want her to waste her energy.

"He doesn't . . . want kids. He . . . never did." Then she choked on her cough for several minutes, which always sounded so scary and was obviously painful. I had learned not to coddle her in the midst of a coughing fit; she didn't like it. Instead, I grabbed some Kleenex and a paper bag. Sometimes she coughed so hard, she threw up. This happened frequently, especially when she got excited or worked up. She hated when her girlfriends got dissed, especially her beloved ones, like Sasha. I didn't say anything, content that she was breathing at all. She sat back and regained her composure.

"And anyway, he moved out again and she's . . . a mess." She coughed a few times more and then proceeded. "She's been crying for three days straight . . . What the crap . . . ? What's wrong with these . . . guys? Anyway . . . I wouldn't trade places with her for . . . anything!" she said, rolling her eyes.

I looked up at her, stunned, remembering her intense longing to be loved by a man. "Not even like this," she said, gesturing toward herself.

A week or so later, Naomi was dying as three of us held her, counting the seconds between her breaths as they spread further and further apart—ten seconds, fifteen seconds, thirty seconds, then forty seconds, then no more breath . . . and like that, she was gone. I immediately burst into song, remembering her departing wish that whoever was near her at the time would sing her to the other side. We all began singing her favorite song, "All you need is love." And, with all our hearts, we watched her amazing, brief, fragile, brave life pass before us.

Changing Hindsight to Insight

Naomi was our very own heroine. For many of us, she changed and touched our lives in a way that will never be forgotten. For me, Naomi was a beacon of courage who walked her talk. She reminded us that every day is a gift, and not to take anything—not even your breath—for granted. Her life and death have changed me unequivocally, and I am grateful beyond words for the gift she was in my world.

I thought I knew what Naomi meant that day when she told me she wouldn't trade places with her broken-hearted girlfriend. I thought she meant that she would rather die of cancer than go through the heartache that love could deliver. That revelation was how this story would have ended. Instead, Naomi came to me in a dream weeks later, with a gift, an incredible gift for us all. She came to me and said that what she wouldn't trade—for any man or anyone or even health—was the self-love, self-awareness, her path to The Divine, what she found inside herself.

After everything she had endured, fought for and railed against—all her years of soul searching and spiritual questing; learning the countless, priceless lessons of caring for herself and the blessings that self-love brings with it; even coming to know God, The Divine, in a way some of us may never know—it was plain to her that she wouldn't give up herself, what she had come to find, for anything. In some way her cancer forced her to love herself, to commit to herself, and to further develop her connection to The Divine—all of which helped her to more fully develop discernment and bring the truly sacred back to sex and love. After all this, she wouldn't give it up for an unconscious, unhealthy, unfulfilling relationship. She knew a truly great relationship does, in fact, begin within; and she wouldn't trade her hard-won wisdom for anything less!

COUNTING BREATHS

Shortly after Naomi's death, a friend shared with me a story about how she, too, had the privilege to sit beside her girlfriend as she passed to the other side. We talked about all they had taught us, how we had both become less frightened and more committed to our lives, and how we were blessed to know them. What struck me most about her story was what she shared about the last three hours of her friend's life.

She said the doctor had just told those who had gathered around her friend's bedside that it would only be a matter of hours before she would pass. And when she heard this, she took her friend's hand, bringing her attention to the rise and fall of her chest. She promptly began to count her friend's breaths over the next hour, in a tender effort to calculate how many breaths she had left. She concluded that, given what the doctor said, she had somewhere in the neighborhood of 1,400 breaths left; she was keeping count, honoring each one. As she did so, something occurred to her that had she had never considered before: she, too, had a finite number of breaths, calculable just the same.

This inextricably brought her face-to-face with her own mortality. She saw that one of the most profound gifts her girlfriend was leaving her was a powerful question. As she watched her beloved friend's fragile, precious, impermanent life slip away, she asked herself the question that I now offer you: How many breaths do you have, and how will you spend them now?

Chapter Eleven

Suggested Reading and Other Great Resources

I have created a CD series that is designed to teach you the profound practice I described in this book, in great detail. It's called *THRIVE: How to Wake Up and Stay Awake—Seven Essential Truths for Revealing Your Secret, Sacred Self.*

If you want an entertaining read, my first book, *Skinny, Tan, and Rich: Unveiling the Myth,* could forever change what you think "having it all" really means.

You can get both the book and the CD by clicking www.maryannelive.com. You can also email me questions, read my blog, check out my free teleseminars, and listen to my live radio interviews with experts including John Gray, Dawna Markova, Gabrielle Roth, Joan Borysenko, Warren Farrell, Gay Hendricks, and Lisa Nichols.

Some of my other favorite books

Atwood, Nina. *Temptations of the Single Girl.* Tucson, AZ: Wheatmark, 2007.

Boryesenko, Joan, Ph.D. *Your Soul's Compass.* Carlsbad, CA: Hay House, 2007.

Eisler, Riane. *The Chalice and the Blade: Our History, Our Future.* San Francisco: Berrett-Koehler, 1998.

——. *The Power of Partnership: Seven Relationships That Will Change Your Life.* San Francisco: Berrett-Koehler, 2003.

Farrell, Dr. Warren. *Why Men Are the Way They Are.* New York: McGraw-Hill, 1986.

——. *Women Can't Hear What Men Don't Say.* New York: Tarcher/Putnam, 1999.

Garchik, Leah. *Real Life Romance: Everyday Wisdom.* San Francisco: Chronicle Books, 2008.

Hawkins, David. *Power vs. Force: The Hidden Determinants of Human Behavior.* Carlsbad, CA: Hay House, 2002.

Hay, Louise. *Heal Your Body.* Carlsbad, CA: Hay House, 1976.

Hogan, Eve. *Intellectual Foreplay.* Alameda, CA: Hunter House 2000.

——. *How to Love your Marriage.* Alameda, CA: Hunter House, 2006.

Houston, Jean. *A Passion for the Possible: A Guide to Realizing Your True Potential.* New York: HarperCollins, 1997.

Kipfer, Barbara Anne. *Four Thousand Questions for Getting to Know Anyone and Everyone.* New York: Random House, 2004.

Lama Surya Das. *The Big Questions: How to Find Your Own Answers to Life's Essential Mysteries.* Pennsylvania, PA: RodaleBooks, 2007.

Long, Barry. *To Woman in Love: A Book of Letters.* London: Barry Long Books, 1994.

Markova, Dawna. *Spot of Grace: Remarkable Stories of How You Do Make a Difference.* Novato, CA: New World Library, 2008.

Miller, Alice. *Drama of the Gifted Child.* New York: Basic Books, 1981.

——. *The Truth Will Set You Free.* New York: Basic Books, 2001.

Moore, Thomas. *Care of the Soul.* New York: HarperCollins, 1992.

Osho. *The Book of the Secrets.* New York: St. Martin's Press, 1998.

Pease, Allan. *Why Men Don't Have A Clue & Women Always Need More Shoes!* New York: Broadway Books, 2004.

Roland, Allen, Ph.D. *Radical Therapy: Surrender to Love and Heal Yourself in Seven Sessions.* Novato, CA: Origin Press, 2001.

Roth, Gabrielle. *Maps to Ecstasy.* Novato, CA: New World Library, 1998.

Samuelson, Elliot, J.D. *The Unmarried Couple's Legal Survival Guide.* New Jersey: Citadel, 1997.

Sri Nisargdatta Maharaj. *I Am That.* Durham, NC: Acorn Press, 1988.

Thomashauer, Regena. *Mama Gena's School of Womanly Arts.* New York: Simon & Schuster, 2003.

Tickle, Naomi. *You Can Read a Face Like a Book.* California: Daniels Publishing, 2003.

Wilbur, Ken. *A Brief History of Everything.* Boston: Shambhala 1996.

Williamson, Marianne. *A Return to Love: Reflections on the Principles of "A Course in Miracles".* New York: HarperCollins, 1992

Yalom, Irvin. *Staring at the Sun: Overcoming the Fear of Death.* San Francisco: Jossey-Bass, 2008.

Sources for "Statistics on Intimate Violence" (page xxii)

1. The National Clearinghouse for the Defense of Battered Women, Washington, D.C., 2006.
2. Ibid.
3. Ibid.
4. Ibid.
5. U.S. Dept. of Justice, Office of Justice Programs, "Intimate Partner Violence," 2004.
6. "Findings from the National Violence Against Women Survey," US Department of Justice, 2000.
7. National Violence Against Women Survey, U.S. Dept. of Health & Human Services, 2003.
8. Whitehead, Barbara, and David Popenoe, *The State of Our Unions* Rutgers University, 2004.
9. Kaiser Family Foundation HIV/AIDS fact sheet, October 2008.
10. Study by Sara Forhan, M.D., M.P.H. Center for Disease Control, March 2008.
11. Center for Disease Control, Suicide fact sheet, 2008.